T0311742

Cambridge Elements

Elements in Magic
edited by
Marion Gibson
University of Exeter

'RITUAL LITTER' REDRESSED

Ceri Houlbrook
University of Hertfordshire

CAMBRIDGE
UNIVERSITY PRESS

CAMBRIDGE
UNIVERSITY PRESS

University Printing House, Cambridge CB2 8BS, United Kingdom

One Liberty Plaza, 20th Floor, New York, NY 10006, USA

477 Williamstown Road, Port Melbourne, VIC 3207, Australia

314–321, 3rd Floor, Plot 3, Splendor Forum, Jasola District Centre,
New Delhi – 110025, India

103 Penang Road, #05–06/07, Visioncrest Commercial, Singapore 238467

Cambridge University Press is part of the University of Cambridge.

It furthers the University's mission by disseminating knowledge in the pursuit of education, learning, and research at the highest international levels of excellence.

www.cambridge.org
Information on this title: www.cambridge.org/9781108949644
DOI: 10.1017/9781108954761

First published 2022

A catalogue record for this publication is available from the British Library.

ISBN 978-1-108-94964-4 Paperback
ISSN 2732-4087 (online)
ISSN 2732-4079 (print)

'Ritual Litter' Redressed

Elements in Magic

DOI: 10.1017/9781108954761
First published online: April 2022

Ceri Houlbrook
University of Hertfordshire

Author for correspondence: Ceri Houlbrook, c.houlbrook@herts.ac.uk

Abstract: Ritual deposition is not an activity that many people in the Western world would consider themselves participants of. The enigmatic beliefs and magical thinking that led to the deposition of swords in watery places and votive statuettes in temples, for example, may feel irrelevant to the modern day. However, it could be argued that ritual deposition is a more widespread feature now than in the past, with folk assemblages – from roadside memorials and love-lock bridges to wishing fountains and coin trees – emerging prolifically worldwide. Despite these assemblages being as much the result of ritual activity as historically deposited objects, they are rarely given the same academic attention or heritage status. Besides exploring the nature of ritual deposition in the contemporary West, and the beliefs and symbolism behind various assemblages, this Element examines the heritage of the modern-day deposit, promoting a renegotiation of the pejorative term 'ritual litter'.

Keywords: ritual litter, folk assemblage, ritual, magical thinking, heritage

ISBNs: 9781108949644 (PB), 9781108954761 (OC)
ISSNs: 2732-4087 (online), 2732-4079 (print)

Contents

Introduction

Inverted commas can reveal a lot. Their use in the title of this Element, *'Ritual Litter' Redressed*, was conscious and deliberate. When the term 'ritual litter' appears within the pages of other books and journals, it is often similarly accompanied by those telltale inverted commas. First given serious consideration in 2003 by anthropologist Jenny Blain and archaeologist Robert Wallis as part of their 'Sacred Sites, Contested Rites/Rights Project', which explored contemporary Pagan engagements with archaeological sites (see forthcoming discussions), the term was offered as 'So-called "ritual litter"' (Wallis & Blain, 2003: 309). And since entering academic parlance, later writers have adopted the same grammatical strategy of presentation (cf. Blain & Wallis, 2004: 241; Rountree, 2006: 100; Bishop, 2016: 44). This is a strategy that marks the term 'ritual litter' as complex, provisional, questionable, or downright problematic. It is also a strategy that distances it from the author. Those two inverted commas represent our hands being held up in both apology and defence: *we're sorry, we know the term is contentious, we didn't coin it, don't blame us.*

Beginning with a definition would seem a logical first step, but 'ritual litter' is as ambiguous a categorization as it is a slippery term. Breaking it into its constituent parts only makes it harder to grasp. What is ritual? Scholars, particularly archaeologists and anthropologists, have been grappling with this question for decades, and a thorough investigation is far beyond the scope of this Element – although a brief overview is necessary. The *Oxford Dictionary of English* (2021) proposes various definitions, from 'The prescribed form or order of religious or ceremonial rites' to 'repeated actions or patterns of behaviour having significance within a particular social group' and simply 'habitual, customary'. Certainly, the term has altered in use through the centuries. 'Instinctively most archaeologists feel they know what ritual is', writes Joanna Brück, 'but, on closer inspection, the picture becomes rather less clear' (2007: 284). Ritual is often 'identified by default'; when an action appears non-functional or beyond rational explanation, it is labelled ritual (Bender, Hamilton, & Tilley, 1997: 148).

To avoid this lacklustre form of identification, many scholars have attempted to pin the term down by proposing definitions. Anthropologist Don Handelman declares these definitions 'unremarkable, noncommittal, and innocuous' (1990: 11), but they do demonstrate some commonalities. Most focus on the physical and symbolic aspects of a practice in their designation of ritual. Robert Bocock defines the term as *'bodily action in relation to symbols'* (1974: 36, emphasis in original), and Susanna Rostas centres on 'a degree of corporeal performativity' in her definition (1998: 92). Some scholars describe formalism, stylization, and repetition as the integral aspects of ritual (Fernandez, 1965: 912; Myerhoff, 1997: 199), while others designate sacred elements and intended preternatural results. Edward Shils, for example, describes ritual as 'a pattern of symbolic actions for renewing contact with the sacred' (1966: 447), while Handelman defines it as an event that 'makes recourse to paranatural, mystical powers' (1990: 5). So there are commonalities, yes, but no clear-cut definition. And as Moore and Myerhoff assert, this 'looseness of the concept of ritual … is a serious obstacle to investigation of the subject' (1997: 21). For the purposes of clarity, this Element defines ritual as follows (whilst acknowledging it is far from comprehensive): intentional, stylized, performative activities that draw on symbolism to make recourse to mystical or preternatural powers.

What of the second word in our slippery term: 'litter'? This undoubtedly refers to material objects linked to ritual activity, but official definitions are vague as to the level of negativity implied by the word 'litter'. 'Odds and ends, fragments and leavings lying about', offers the *Oxford Dictionary of English* (2021), which is quite harmless, but the addition of the terms 'rubbish; a state of confusion or untidiness; a disorderly accumulation of things lying about', gives a less innocuous impression. 'Rubbish', after all, is more straightforwardly defined as 'Waste material … rejected and useless matter of any kind … Material that is considered worthless, unimportant, or of very poor quality: trash'. 'Rubbish' is an explicitly negative label, and the *Cambridge Dictionary* (2021) defines 'litter' as 'small pieces of rubbish that have been left lying on the ground in public places'.

If the term 'litter' is intended to empirically describe the leaving of objects in public places in relation to ritual activities, then there may be little distinguishing them from objects labelled 'structured deposits'. This is an archaeological term coined by Richards and Thomas in their 1984 paper 'Ritual Activity and Structured Deposition in Later Neolithic Wessex'. It is a concept anchored within the archaeology of ritual, which Richards and Thomas describe as 'formalised repetitive actions which may be detected archaeologically through a highly structured mode of deposition' (1984: 215). By 'structured mode', they mean placed in a way that suggests deliberate deposition, and this constitutes a vast body of material, from prehistoric weapons deposited in rivers and coins left at Roman temples to rags tied around trees and bras hung on fences. Variously termed ritual deposits, votives, ex-votos, and folk assemblages, these are all objects that have been deposited in public places as part of ritual activities. The empirical term 'ritual litter' could apply to most of these items and would therefore be almost interchangeable with the immense subject of structured deposition. However, this Element is not viewing the term 'ritual litter' as an empirical description but interpreting it as a negative appraisal of material culture. For the purposes of this Element, therefore, 'ritual litter' refers to that subcategory of structured deposits that are viewed as problematic.

Considering how the term is used has been vital to this decision. In 2003, for example, Wallis and Blain observed that 'So-called "ritual litter" is an increasing problem at many sacred sites' (2003: 309), while anthropologist Kathryn Rountree opined in 2006 that 'ritual litter' is a term employed 'by those inclined to disapprove of their deposition' (2006: 100). The term often identifies the negative interpretation of ritual deposits. But what fuels these negative interpretations? What causes these structured deposits to be viewed as problematic? To be treated as rubbish: 'rejected and useless . . . worthless, unimportant, or of very poor quality'? There is no straightforward answer.

Is it a matter of age? Objects assembled in relation to ritual activities in prehistoric and historic contexts – from Bronze Age river deposits to votive offerings on the Athenian acropolis – do not tend to be viewed as unimportant or problematic. They are 'ritual deposits' rather than 'ritual litter'. Is this a case of age validating the value of something? As Sefryn Penrose observes, 'the older something becomes the more important it tends to be thought' (2007: 13). In his research on arborglyphs (tree graffiti), Troy Lovata notes the heritage value given to historic examples of such graffiti, viewed as worthy of study and preservation, in contrast to contemporary examples, which are disapproved of and prohibited (2015: 95). This notion of age value may go some way in explaining the conceptual difference between 'ritual deposit' and 'ritual litter'. However, as this Element will demonstrate, some historic examples have been viewed as problematic. The personal possessions, such as clothing and jewellery, ritually deposited at the Catholic shrine to Our Lady of Lourdes in Lourdes, France (see Section 3), were viewed negatively by clerics in the nineteenth century, who commissioned people to remove material offerings and keep the grotto 'tidy' (Notermans & Jansen, 2011: 176–7). While in the twenty-first century, people have been actively encouraged to throw coins into wishing wells or attach love-locks (padlocks typically inscribed with the depositors' names or initials, locked in place to ritually declare romantic attachment) to particular structures (Houlbrook, 2015a: 183, 2021: 126–34). So it is not always a clear-cut case of 'old is good, new is bad'.

Is the problematic perception of some assemblages due more to their size than to their age? Are ritual deposits identified as 'litter' when they reach a certain quantity? This is no doubt true in some cases, but not all large assemblages are viewed negatively. Jordan Conley describes how votives have 'littered sites' through history, seen in 'excess at sanctuaries, shrines, and tombs' (2020: 47), and yet here the verb 'litter' does not necessarily indicate the noun 'litter'. Is it perhaps more to do with the nature of the object? Does having a higher monetary or perceived aesthetic value prevent a ritual deposit from being deemed 'litter'? Again, this is true in some cases. But, as demonstrated in research conducted on 'The Votives Project', objects can be cheap and mass-produced without being interpreted as worthless or problematic.[1]

Interestingly, Hilary Joyce Bishop, writing about Mass Rocks (natural, remote sites where Catholic Mass was held during Penal times) in Uíbh Laoghaire, Ireland, implies it is an absence of inherent sacrality that designates a ritual deposit 'litter'. 'The range of votive offerings deposited at sacred spaces can vary enormously', she writes. 'It can range from "ritual litter" such as flowers, coins, candles, tea light holders and other such objects to the deposition of objects already considered sacred such as stones and crystals' (2016: 44). The implication here is that the ritually recycled object – that which was not *already considered sacred* before deposition – is more likely to be deemed 'litter'. The coin that was currency before being hammered into a tree. The rag that was clothing before being tied around a branch. The teddy bear that was a toy before being placed on a public memorial. However, this distinction is difficult to maintain. The prehistoric weapons ritually deposited in watery places, as described by archaeologist Richard Bradley (1990), for example, were not originally crafted as ritual deposits but as weapons, and yet the fact they were ritually recycled does not equate them to 'litter' in the modern gaze. While some contemporary love-locks were created specifically as ritual deposits, crafted in the shape of love hearts with no accompanying key, they can only really be used in the love-lock ritual. And yet so many love-lock assemblages have been derisively judged 'rubbish'.

Is it more about the nature of the place of deposition, rather than the object itself? Rountree observes that people 'might light a candle or write a prayer and deposit it in a special place in a church without the candle or prayer being termed "ritual litter"' (2006: 100). The difference, she argues, is that churches are generally seen as 'sacred places'. It does not follow, though, that objects deposited in explicitly acknowledged 'sacred places' are never viewed negatively. As we have already seen, items left in the Marian grotto in Lourdes were and are treated as litter. Conversely, some ritual deposits placed in seemingly mundane public spaces are not treated as litter.

One example of this is the Canang Sari (Figure 1). Consisting primarily of leaves, flowers, food, and incense, these neat packages are deposited on a daily basis by Balinese Hindus, as sustenance for, and thanks to, the spirits. As Emily Martin, who conducted fieldwork for her undergraduate anthropology thesis in

---

[1] For example, Maria Anna De Lucia Brolli and Jacopo Tabolli (2015) discuss the 100 iron keys found deposited at the ancient sanctuary of Monte Li Santi-Le Rote at Narce, Italy, as valuable finds, while E.-J. Graham (2014) explores the possibilities of ('cheap') wax figurines of gods deposited in Graeco-Roman shrines.

Figure 1 The disarranged offerings of the Canang Sari at the end of the day,
Bali, Indonesia, 2013 (photograph by the author)

Bali, observed, 'offerings are placed everywhere': at busy road junctions, on the
beach, on the street in front of houses and shops, placed strategically so that
'those walking by are forced to look at them' (Martin, 2018: 70). Lindsey
Siadis, who conducted postgraduate research on the phenomenon, also noted
their prevalence, declaring that she 'found it highly remarkable that these
offerings were often put in places where they would most likely be run over'
(2014: 31). Those not run over are often eaten by animals, such as dogs or
monkeys. Though beautifully crafted, after a day of road and foot traffic, these
offerings do begin to resemble disorderly accumulations of waste material, all
the more so for the modern trend in including packaged sweets. They begin to
look like rubbish.

However, these ubiquitous contemporary offerings of low economic value, which are placed on the ground to be trampled and scavenged, *littering* the street, are not viewed as ritual litter. They are actively encouraged by communities and religious authorities, with the government reportedly distributing pamphlets that specify the ingredients and frequency of offerings and temple loudspeakers reminding Hindus to make their offerings (Martin, 2018: 99). In fact, both Martin and Siadis comment on the immense pressure Balinese women in particular feel to make and publicly deposit the correct ritual offerings. The fact that many of these offerings are made in the street does not negate their ritual value, which again calls into question the theory that deposits made in non-sacred spaces tend to be classed as ritual litter. Notions of 'sacred place' and 'non-sacred space' are notoriously subjective anyway.[2]

So why are Balinese Canang Sari encouraged as ritual deposits, while in other cases elsewhere in the world, ubiquitous contemporary offerings of low economic value are problematized as litter? Is it a matter of permission and authority? The Balinese government approve of these offerings because they are an integral element of Indonesian Hinduism (Martin, 2018: 71–3). Conversely, many Roman Catholic clerics did not (and do not) view material offerings made at the Marian grotto in Lourdes as a prescribed practice of their religion; they are therefore viewed and treated by authorities as ritual litter: prohibited, removed, and largely disposed of (Notermans & Jansen, 2011). The defining characteristic of 'ritual litter' may therefore be objects ritually deposited *without the approval or permission of authorities*.

Who constitutes the authorities, however, is also subjective. Landowners, site managers, spiritual leaders, heritage specialists, archaeologists, and ritual practitioners – not to mention members of the general public – all claim some authority in how a space or place is used. It is rare for all stakeholders to be in agreement. Therefore, what are 'small pieces of rubbish that have been left lying on the ground' to one group may be a 'sacred assemblage of ritual deposits' to another (Rountree, 2006: 100). 'Ritual litter' thus proves to be as subjective a term as it is elusive. This subjectivity – while making a neat definition impossible – proves central to the concept of 'ritual litter' and is hence a recurring theme throughout this Element.

---

[2] Geographer Della Dora discusses how 'sacred space' is difficult to define: 'Sacred space eludes us. It stretches our senses. It problematizes traditional binary distinctions, such as those between the spiritual and the material, the invisible and the visible, the eternal and the contingent. Where do the boundaries of the sacred lie? Is sacred space an ontological given or, a social construction? Is it a portion of territory or the product of a set of embodied performances? Is it permanent or ephemeral?' (2011: 165).

This Element does not claim to offer a comprehensive look at 'ritual litter' worldwide. Such an endeavour would require a far larger word count and knowledge of many languages (perhaps a future project for an international group of researchers). Nor is it within this Element's remit to tackle questions of ritual continuity or debates over the broader uses of, and rights to, sites. What this Element does offer are some examples, largely from Europe and North America, of ritual deposits identified by at least one group of stakeholders as problematic. They range from Neopagan offerings made at Stone Age sites in Finland to roadside shrines in New Mexico, from coins thrown from the peak of a Californian mountain to a vast assemblage of love-locks in Paris. These examples are chosen to illustrate the wide variety both in the forms of deposited objects and in how such objects are treated.

Section 1 considers the people and places of contemporary ritual deposition, exploring who makes such offerings and at what types of sites. Section 2 takes a contemporary archaeological perspective, unpicking the material culture of the different types of deposits and asking why particular items were chosen and what their intended purposes or messages were. Section 3 considers how and why such objects have been interpreted as problematic by certain stakeholders and how they – along with the sites that accommodate them – have subsequently been treated. Section 4 concludes by examining the cultural heritage value of purportedly problematic ritual deposits. Examples are presented of particular individuals and groups who have recognized this value and employed a variety of methods to preserve or record the tangible cultural heritage of what some dismiss as litter.

The aim throughout this Element is to demonstrate both the prevalence and inevitable plurality of 'ritual litter'. Taking the deposited object as a focal point, it details the challenges it has raised and the opportunities it has proffered. Most significantly, the Element explores what our responses to 'ritual litter' reveal about our relationships with the past, the places we experience, and the people we share them with.

1 The Places and the People

Coins and crystals. Rags and teddy bears. Flowers and human ashes. Virgin Mary statuettes and Barbie dolls. Padlocks and 'I Voted' stickers. Other than their portability, these objects have little in common in terms of their material culture. And yet they are all examples of unsanctioned ritual deposits. The aim of this section is to consider why. After all, conscious decisions and motivations were behind their selections, whether they were a matter of convenience, disposability, some perceived significance within the materiality of the object, cultural associations surrounding the type of object, or more personal associations.

As ancient historian Robin Osborne asks: 'Why did anyone think that depositing this or that particular object or group of objects was an appropriate way of marking or establishing communications with transcendent powers?' (2004: 7). Some deposited objects were originally crafted *as* deposited objects, such as medieval pilgrim badges or statuettes of deities. The vast majority of 'ritual litter', however, are the ordinary, mundane objects that have been ritually recycled or, to use Osborne's word, 'converted' into ritual objects (2004: 2). This section, therefore, surveys the various types of objects that could be classed as 'ritual litter' and considers potential reasons behind their selection as deposits. It is beyond the remit of this Element to delve into the broader contexts of the places at which they are deposited, which range from prehistoric sites of archaeological value to contemporary bridges, from path-side tree boles of no obvious significance to roadside sites of fatal car accidents. It is also beyond the Element's scope to detail the myriad (and often indistinct) groups of depositors, with the multitude of beliefs, aims, and politics that may motivate them. Both are, however, necessary to explore in this section, to provide context for the central focus of the next section: the objects themselves.

The term 'ritual litter' is most explicitly applied to objects deposited at sites of prehistoric or historic significance, where they are seen as particularly problematic because they can compromise archaeological integrity. It is unsurprising that such contemporary deposits are so often made at such places, given their popularity as stages or centres of contemporary spiritual practices.[3] These places include the globally high profile, some of which feature on the UN Educational, Scientific and Cultural Organization (UNESCO) World Heritage List: the prehistoric stone circle of Stonehenge, for example, or the pre-Columbian cultural complex of Chaco Culture National Historical Park, New Mexico. But deposition also often occurs at less internationally known sites: prehistoric dolmen in Brittany, France; historic Sámi ritual sites in Finland; Christian holy wells in Ireland; and Neolithic burial chambers in Wales (de la Torre, 2018; Gibby, 2018). Wallis and Blain (2003) estimate that the phenomenon of large-scale ritual deposition at such sites rose in the 1980s and continued rising into the 2000s.

Writing in 2019 of contemporary deposits left at sacred spaces in Finland and Estonia, Jonuks and Äikäs made the following observation:

---

[3] Jutta Leskovar and Raimund Karl (2018) have edited a very useful multi-contributor volume on modern spiritual practices at archaeological sites, which demonstrates this popularity.

> Deposits could be divided into three groups: those connected with old tradi-
> tions and revitalising old folk beliefs, those that seem to stem from ritual
> creativity and build new ways of communication with sacred places, and
> finally deposits that are left for touristic purposes by copying the already
> existing phenomena. (2019: 40)

These three groups, however, are far from distinct, as Jonuks and Äikäs recognize. There is much overlap between them. The line between 'old traditions' and
'ritual creativity' is particularly hazy, especially given the ambiguities and
contestations surrounding the concept of 'old traditions'. An illustrative
example is the holy well.

Found globally, these sites of holy healing waters were and are believed
sacred by their associations with Christian saints – who may in some cases have
supplanted pre-Christian spirits or deities (Foley, 2011, 2013). In an empirical
study of representative wells across Ireland, which accommodates an estimated
3,000 holy wells, Foley observes objects that evidence 'complex and ambiva-
lent histories' (2013: 48) and a 'heterogeneous set of healing (spiritual and
practical) practices' (2013: 47). These objects include rags used in healing
rituals (see Section 2), crutches left in thanks for a miraculous cure, Mass
cards, photographs of loved ones, and red ribbons believed to have been
deposited by Wiccan practitioners (Figure 2). The author's own empirical
studies of Irish holy wells reveal a similar (sometimes seemingly incompatible)
concoction of objects. At St Brendan's holy well at Clonfert, County Galway,
a holy water container in the shape of the Virgin Mary lay next to a Barbie doll
(Figure 3). Not far from both were a Buddha statuette, a cluster of inhalers,
many rosary beads, and a dustpan and brush. As Rackard, O'Callaghan, and
Joyce, note: 'Some holy wells look like shrines to recycling' (2001: 12).

Such jarringly mismatched assemblages lead Foley to make the following
observation:

> As pilgrimage settings are invariably spaces of change and movement (of
> people, objects and meanings), new uses and identities, associated with groups
> of difference such as neo-pagans and Travellers emerge. These are in turn
> shaped by independently developed contemporary cultural practices so that
> they have increasingly become spaces of memory and mourning as well.
> Ironically for sites that are of their essence, organic, grounded and free, holy
> wells have been subject to a surprising number of contestations shaped by
> a series of 'gazes' including the religious, colonial and medical where they
> have at different times been suppressed, overwritten and dismissed. (2013: 49)

Similar complexities and contestations surrounding the distinction between
'old traditions' and 'ritual creativity' are evident in *sieiddit*, offering places
used by the indigenous Sámi peoples of Finland, Sweden, Norway, and the

Figure 2 A cluttered assemblage of photographs, rosary beads, rags, and statuettes at St Brigid's Well, Liscannor, County Clare, Ireland, 2012 (photograph by the author)

Figure 3 A Barbie doll accompanies the Virgin Mary amidst the offerings at St Brendan's Tree, Clonfert, County Galway, Ireland, 2012 (photograph by the author)

Kola Peninsula. Conducting research at such sites in Northern Norway, Spangen and Äikäs note the likelihood of such items as felled reindeer antlers having been ritually deposited by members of Sámi communities. They also remark on the reluctance among Sámi peoples to 'admit to any sort of continuous offering tradition', which Spangen and Äikäs attribute to the history of persecution of the Sámi religion. Instead, such ritual deposits are identified as offerings made in respect of their *ancestors'* beliefs, rather than their own (2020: 317). Conversely, many ritual deposits are made at historic *sieiddit* sites by non-Sámi peoples, which are explicitly connected with the depositors' spiritual beliefs: those of contemporary Pagans. At such sites, tenth-century bones, seventeenth-century jewellery, and nineteenth-century coins can rub shoulders with twenty-first-century tea-light candles (Äikäs, 2015; Äikäs & Ahola, 2020).

Modern-day ritual deposition at archaeological and historic sites do tend to be attributed to the spiritual practices of contemporary Pagans.[4] The majority of Leskovar and Karl's 2018 edited volume on *Archaeological Sites as Space for Modern Spiritual Practice* explores the activities of Pagans, as did Wallis and Blain's 'Sacred Sites, Contested Rites/Rights Project', which began in 2001. Blain and Wallis (2004, 2007; Wallis and Blain 2003) detail how increasing numbers of Pagans have been identifying ancient sites as sacred, performing activities there that involve the offering of ritual deposits. Perceived continuity is central here, ancient sites being viewed as prominent markers of the pre-Christian belief systems that inspire contemporary Paganism (Doyle White, 2018: 182).

For most modern Pagan sites, continuity is more believed than archaeologically evidenced. Doyle White suggests it is partly the associations of such sites with folklore, such as the Rollright Stones' folkloric link with witches, that have led to their embrace by Pagan groups: 'prehistoric monuments', he notes, 'have been regularly reused by people from later societies, and as a result have accrued a great deal of folk belief surrounding them' (2018: 188). Despite the ambiguity (and often contested nature) of ritual continuity at such sites, they are seen as no less sacred by contemporary practitioners. And, as Blain and Wallis observe, 'For some pagans, these offerings forge and strengthen links with sites, and honour wights, goddesses or some other local spirits' (2004: 246), while Jonuks and Äikäs note that the deposition of offerings can form part of the veneration of nature (2019: 8). Human

---

[4] Following Ethan Doyle White's advice, upper-case 'Paganism' is used here to refer to modern practitioners of new religious movements inspired by the lower-case 'pagan' belief systems of pre-Christian Europe. 'Paganism' is often used interchangeably with 'Neopaganism', which Doyle White has identified as potentially problematic (2018: 182).

geographer James Thurgill, who conducted fieldwork at the Ankerwycke Yew, Berkshire, a focal point of Pagan ritual due to being one of the oldest trees in Britain, describes the 'trinketisation' of the tree with ribbons, crystals, flowers, and candles, as a possible method of 'payments of love and respect to the spirit of the place, its genius loci, and in doing so there exists the hope that such an act can bring about an affective change to a space outside of the tree' (2014: 181–2).

However, it must be emphasized here (as it will also be in Section 3) that there is no uniformity of Pagan engagement with archaeological sites. As Blain and Wallis stress, '"pagans" do not form a unified whole' (2007: 59). Paganism is a very broad umbrella term for a vast and vastly diverse group of people worldwide, consisting of many different branches (such as Druidry, wicca, neoshamanism), each with their own subgroups of individuals, each with their own sets of personal beliefs. Even practitioners from the same Pagan community can view and treat the same site differently. Some people practice prescribed activities organized by a group,[5] while others follow what Blain and Wallis describe as 'individual divine inspiration for whatever practices seem appropriate at the time' (2007: 27, 42).

It is not, however, only Pagans who leave unsanctioned ritual deposits at archaeological sites – and as will be explored in Section 3, many Pagans choose not to leave ritual offerings, viewing them as problematic. Many objects are left by another group: tourists.[6] Such objects generally receive less academic attention but are no less prevalent, in some cases perceived as having been influenced by Pagan activities. The distinction between Pagan offering and tourist deposit is not always materially evident, as Jonuks and Äikäs, writing of contemporary Pagan sites in Estonia and Finland, acknowledge. However, this does not prevent them from interpreting some objects as 'left for touristic purposes by copying the already existing phenomena' (2019: 40). Examples of this include plastic bags, Christmas decorations, and stockings deposited in (subjectively poor) imitation of rags and ribbons offered by Pagan communities (2019: 19). Imitation is viewed as the key motivator here. A tourist visits an archaeological site, witnesses contemporary offerings made by Pagan depositors, and decides to add to the accumulation themselves.

---

[5] As described, for example, in Thurgill, 2014: 155–82.

[6] Much past literature has focused on the creation or performance of culture for tourists rather than by tourists, and Bruner notes the ethnographer's tendency to omit tourists from their studies altogether: 'a purposeful ignoring of that which is present but that ethnography finds embarrassing' (2005: 8). However, some research has focused on the culture of tourists themselves, such as MacCannell's seminal 1976 *The Tourist: A new theory of the leisure class* and Urry's 2002 *The Tourist Gaze*.

Imitation, so central to learning processes and often the driving force behind collective behaviour, is a widely acknowledged dissemination mechanism within ritual practices (Houlbrook, 2015b). I see others participate and therefore participate myself; I see *how* others participate and therefore participate this way myself. Accumulations of deposited objects, identified by folklorist Jack Santino (2004) as 'folk assemblages', grow because they invite spontaneous and imitative participation from others. Lynne McNeill (2007) identifies these growths as 'serial collaborative creations', chain assemblages in the sense that they rely on the imitative deposition of past and future participants. However, not all imitative tourist deposits are inspired by Pagan precursors, and most do not occur at archaeological sites. Some assemblages of unsanctioned ritual deposits are created (or wholly perpetuated) by tourists, defined here as anyone travelling beyond their community for pleasure as opposed to business.

Coin trees are one such example. As explored in more depth elsewhere by the author, these are trees, logs, or stumps, into which people have embedded coins in exchange for wishes or luck. The author has catalogued over 200 across Britain and Ireland. There are some pre-twentieth-century examples of this practice in Scotland and Ireland, where the trees are in close proximity to Christian holy healing wells – and thereby sacred by association. However, the majority of coin trees are contemporary, dating to the 1990s, 2000s, and 2010s (Figure 4; Houlbrook, 2014, 2018a). They do not tend to be in places of known spiritual or ritual significance, largely situated beside well-trodden footpaths in popular woodland areas. Some particularly well-established examples are a large fallen tree along Ingleton Waterfalls Trail, North Yorkshire, which contained more than 40,000 coins at the time it was catalogued by the author in 2012, and a log along a trail leading to Aira Force in the Lake District, Cumbria, with at least 20,000. Based on ethnographic observations, interviews with participants, and correspondence with site managers at forty coin tree sites, it is clear that most of these unsanctioned assemblages were begun by tourists (domestic or international) and that they are continued by tourists. During observations, many walkers were witnessed passing the coin trees, noticing the assemblages of coins, exhibiting surprise, then spontaneously choosing to make their own deposit by using rocks from the ground to hammer their pennies into the trees (Houlbrook, 2015b). Tourists make ritual offerings, and more tourists follow suit.

However, there is no straightforward answer for why a tourist would choose to contribute a ritual deposit to an unsanctioned assemblage. Tourists are another 'group' often inaccurately homogeneously batched. Anyone can be a tourist. The domestic day tripper, the international sightseer, the hiker, the child on a school outing. Their motivations for making a ritual deposit will be as

Figure 4 The densely coined coin tree of Ingleton, Yorkshire, England, 2012 (photograph by the author)

myriad and diverse as they are. For wish-making, for luck, for the sense of participation, for the photo opportunity. Furthermore, the distinction between tourist and spiritual practitioner (e.g. a member of a Pagan community or a Christian pilgrim) may be misleading. Equations between tourists and pilgrims (and mourners – see later), holidays and rituals, the 'secular' pilgrimage and the 'traditional' pilgrimage, having frequently been made, there can be no decisive, impermeable line between spiritual practitioner and tourist.[7] A person can easily be both.

---

[7] Anthropologists Victor and Edith Turner famously observed, 'a tourist is half a pilgrim, if a pilgrim is half a tourist' (1978: 20), whilst Singh notes that pilgrimages have been identified in sociology and anthropology as the earliest form of tourism (2005: 215). See also Eade & Sallnow, 1991; Margry 2008a.

This ambiguity is clearly evident at sites such as Lourdes, France, where a visitor to the Catholic shrine to Our Lady of Lourdes may see themselves as simultaneously a pilgrim and a tourist. The objects they ritually leave at the site, therefore, are both tourist deposits and the offerings of a spiritual practitioner. This is also the case on popular pilgrimage routes. In Bert Groenewoudt's 2017 study of contemporary unsanctioned shrines along the Camino Frances, the most popular route of the Way of St. James (*Camino de Santiago*), which runs from France to Galicia, Spain, it is clearly evident that no strict distinction can be made between the tourist deposit and the spiritual offering. The plastic shoe containing a small statue of the Virgin Mary with Child, the makeshift crosses crafted from twigs, the strips of fabric, the stones sourced on site bearing scratched names, the In Memoriam cards, all speak to a diverse set of visitors with a diverse set of motivations.

Another ambiguous category of ritual depositor is the ostensive pilgrim, a term based on a folkloric concept. Folklorists Linda Dégh and Andrew Vázsonyi (1983) borrowed the word 'ostension' (from the Latin *ostendere*, 'to show') from semiotics to conceptualize the physical enactment – the showing of actions – of fictional narratives. These may be from television and film as well as folklore and legend, and they become subject to ostension when fans enact scenes from within the narrative. The ostensive pilgrim is the fan who travels to a specific destination to enact a scene, perhaps where it was set or filmed: Transylvania for fans of Bram Stoker's *Dracula* or London's King's Cross train station for fans of *Harry Potter*.[8] And the ostensive pilgrim can easily become the ostensive depositor, leaving objects appropriate to the narrative at the site they have visited.

It is ostensive deposition that is behind the assemblages of coins in Rome's Trevi Fountain, the well-known 'tradition' of tossing a coin into the fountain having entered the tourist's consciousness through *Three Coins in the Fountain* (1954), even if the visitor has never seen the film (Caplin, 2000; Clapp, 2009: 54). Ostensive deposition is likewise behind the twenty-first-century love-lock bridge (Houlbrook, 2021). Although there are earlier examples of the ritual deposition of padlocks on public structures, the concept of locking your love onto a bridge became hugely popular following a teenage romance novel. In 2006, Italian novelist Federico Moccia published *Ho voglia di te* (*I Want You*), in which a pair of lovers declare their romantic commitment by attaching a padlock to the Milvio Bridge, Rome (2006: 274–6, translation by Francesca Benetti). This ritual was imitated by

---

[8] See, for example, Light, 2009; Gymnich & Sheunemann, 2017.

the many fans of the novel, and by the time the Milvio Bridge was being filmed for a movie adaptation in 2007, a large assemblage of ostensively deposited padlocks had already formed. Fans who could not visit Rome initiated the custom elsewhere, such as Venice's Rialto Bridge, cementing the custom as a ritual declaration of romantic commitment that spread worldwide as tourists began imitating the fans en masse (see Sections 3 and 4).

A subcategory of the ostensive pilgrim is the ostensive mourner. This mourning occurs when a fictional character (or a person connected with the character, such as a writer or actor) dies. An appropriate site is visited, and an object left in memoriam. If there are enough ostensive mourners, impromptu memorials become established, and assemblages of unsanctioned deposits grow. This occurred at Mermaid Quay, Cardiff, following the 2009 death of character Ianto Jones from BBC science-fiction television series *Torchwood*. At a site close to the fictional headquarters of Torchwood, an assemblage of flowers, notes, photographs, and personal items formed (Beattie, 2014). A similar memorial grew in 2016 close to London's King's Cross train station's Platform 9¾, following the death of actor Alan Rickman who played *Harry Potter* character Severus Snape, while the phone box outside St Bartholomew's Hospital, from which Sherlock Holmes famously jumped in a 2012 episode of BBC's *Sherlock*, quickly filled with messages to Sherlock and prayers for his safety.

It is not only ostensive mourning that leads to unsanctioned ritual deposition. Unofficial memorials – variously referred to as 'makeshift memorials', 'temporary memorials', 'vernacular memorials', 'grassroot memorials', or 'spontaneous shrines'[9] – emerge far more frequently in response to *non*-fictional deaths or tragic events.[10] Erika Doss maintains that 'Links between material culture and mourning are timeless, of course, and the gift giving at spontaneous shrines stems from long-standing materialist practices surrounding the memorialization of the dead' (2006: 298). This 'gift giving' is the unsanctioned ritual deposition, and these spontaneous shrines are the products of their assemblage.

Spontaneous shrines can be devoted to one individual, usually following a sudden and tragic death. The roadside memorial, established at the site of a fatal car accident, is a prime example. Roadside memorials have deep

---

[9] Note Jack Santino's dismissal of the term 'makeshift memorial' as 'condescending and inaccurate' (2004: 369).

[10] Many thanks to Helen Frisby, author of *Traditions of Death and Burial* (2019), and Janine Marriott, Arnos Vale public engagement manager, for their valuable insights into this topic. See also Doss, 2008.

historical roots, particularly in Latin American culture, but it was only in the 1990s that they became common practice across America, Europe, and Australasia (Clark & Franzmann, 2006: 580; Klaasens, Groote, & Huigen, 2009: 188; Dickinson & Hoffmann, 2010: 154; Milošević, 2018: 56; Frisby, 2019: 84). In 1997, folklorist George Monger suggested two primary reasons for their construction: memorialization and warning (1997: 114). On one hand, they are made by the family and friends of the deceased in a ritual act of mourning. In their study of roadside memorials in the Netherlands, Klaasens, Groote, and Huigen observe that such sites, previously anonymous roadsides, are 'transformed into a place with special, even sacred, meanings to the bereaved, as it is the place where their loved one has died' (2009: 187). Continued depositional activity beyond the memorial's original construction, with new mementos added over time by family, friends, and even strangers, fosters a sense of ongoing remembrance (Clark & Franzmann, 2006: 590).

The creation of a site explicitly associated with the deceased and the deposition of material offerings, the memoriam deposits, has long been a significant step in what Sylvia Grider identifies as the 'grieving ritual' (2001: 1). 'Placing a memento', Grider writes, 'gives people a sense of purpose, making them feel less helpless and powerless ... an act as sacred and comforting as lighting a candle at a church altar' (2001: 2), while Milošević describes spontaneous memorialization as 'One of the ways in which society copes, channels and negotiates a traumatic event' (Milošević, 2018: 53). In most Western societies, however, the construction of a roadside shrine is less traditional than lighting a candle at a church altar and may indicate that the mourners who create such shrines desire an alternative to more conventional mourning practices in societies. This would be in keeping with the growing popularity of the custom since the 1990s, in societies where attitudes towards death and religion have shifted, rendering older commemorative practices inadequate and generating the need for new ones (Clark & Franzmann, 2006: 583; Dickinson & Hoffmann, 2010: 165).

In addition to mourning, Monger (1997) identified 'warning' as a reason behind the roadside memorial's construction. The place of the memorial is significant not only because it was where a loved one died – and thus, as Hilary Orange and Paul Graves-Brown note, 'can serve as a focus' (2019: 345) – but also because it was the site of a motoring accident. Their presence, visible to anyone driving past, can therefore serve as a warning to other motorists of the (possibly location specific) hazards of driving (Santino, 2004: 369). Different forms of sudden tragic death are also memorialized this way, and they can equally act as warnings or reflections on other dangers and their related social issues, from knife crime and terrorism (engendering memoriam deposits with patriotic symbolism, such as the American flag) to comments on police brutality (Grider, 2001: 4; Santino, 2004: 369; Frisby, 2019: 84). As Doss notes, 'memorials have the power to stir things up as much as they may smooth them out' (2008: 8).

The individual being memorialized by spontaneous shrines may also be a prominent figure, and the unsanctioned memoriam deposits are made by members of the public. Such figures may have been politicians, such as Pim Fortuyn, whose assassination in 2002 sparked numerous spontaneous shrines across the Netherlands (Klaasens, Groote, & Huigen, 2009: 188). They may have been celebrities, from musicians David Bowie, Freddie Mercury, and Amy Winehouse (Graves-Brown & Orange, 2017; Orange & Graves-Brown, 2019) to athletes such as long-distance runner Steve Prefontaine (Wojcik, 2008). The spontaneous shrines are often set up at sites significant to the deceased, such as where they lived, worked, achieved something, wrote or sang about, or died, and they tend to consist of objects connected to the person (their likes and interests) alongside more conventional memoriam deposits (see Section 2). They are, as Graves-Brown and Orange describe, 'the product of collective and democratic popular activity, as opposed to the numerous official memorials and plaques which commemorate prominent people' (2017: 121). Inherently connected with fan culture, people can travel long distances to visit these shrines and make their offerings, and writing about them in the context of pilgrimages, Peter Jan Margry identifies such sites as places where 'the veneration, glorification, and idolization of secular individuals takes place' (2008a: 37).

Even memoriam deposits placed at official graves (again, often connected to the deceased's likes and interests) can be viewed as unsanctioned. Some are more tolerated than others, such as the pens deposited at the grave of novelist Douglas Adams in Highgate Cemetery, London, or the 'I Voted' stickers at the grave of suffragist Susan B. Anthony in Rochester, New York. Such public figures can become 'secular saints', as Conley observes, 'whose lives and legacies inspire pilgrimages and evoke a certain religiosity' (2020: 46 n). Conley identifies such gravesite deposits as 'ritual votive objects', which are 'central to questions of devotion and remembrance' (2020: 45). Other items are viewed more explicitly as 'litter' and removed, such as the bottles of whiskey and bags of marijuana left at the grave of singer/writer Jim Morrison in Père Lachaise Cemetery, Paris (Margry, 2008b).

Ritual deposits are also frequently left at sites memorializing tragic events that led to multiple fatalities. The sites can include spontaneous shrines, such as the many that materialized in New York following the 9/11 attack (Grider, 2001), in Brussels following the 2016 terrorist attack (Milošević, 2018), and in Manchester following the 2017 attack (Arvanitis, 2019), to name only some. They also include the unofficial assemblages forming at official memorials, such as the 214,000+ objects left by visitors to the Vietnam Veterans Memorial (VVM) in Washington, DC (pers. Janet Folkerts, Museum Curator, National Mall and Memorial Parks). Again, objects range from the conventional memoriam deposit (such as flowers, candles, and letters) to the more personal (see Section 2). As with many of the previous examples, visits to these assemblages are viewed as pilgrimages: as sites for depositing an offering and as sites for observing the offerings of others (Grider, 2001: 4). As sites of grieving and commemoration, but also of 'highly orchestrated performances of mourning', to use Doss's words (2006: 298). The very public, very visible nature of these memorials leads Santino to propose an additional motivating factor behind memoriam deposits: 'a need to demonstrate to an audience one does not know that one participated, that one contributed to this monument, and that one was there, albeit anonymously' (2004: 366).

This desire to materially declare one's presence is potentially (perhaps subconsciously) behind many cases of ritual deposition, even when part of spiritual practices.[11] Each deposit is a personal contribution to a communal piece. Äikäs and Ahola, writing of contemporary offerings at the *sieidi* (indigenous Sámi offering site) of Taatsi, Finland, remark that 'it seems as if they [the depositors] wanted to somehow mark the site' (2020: 173). Granted, most deposits are anonymous, bearing no obvious markers that tangibly and explicitly link them to their depositors (love-locks being an obvious exception, counter to the homogenous coin). But, to the depositor, that object is *theirs*. Jonuks and Äikäs believe that for Pagan depositors in Northern Europe at least, objects can be 'left as a personal sign of a wish' or as a token of their engagement with the site, but this can apply to any depositor, whether they identify primarily as tourist, mourner, pilgrim, or spiritual practitioner (2019: 8). To draw on an archaeological concept, the deposit is entangled with the depositor, in that it becomes metonymically linked with the person through the act of deposition (Thomas, 1991; Weiner, 1992; Fowler, 2005; Hodder, 2012; Houlbrook, 2015c). Such objects are not designed to simply represent the depositor but are intended to *be* the depositor. As archaeologist Chris Tilley writes, the 'thing is the person and the

---

[11] Raimund Karl considers how some spiritual practitioners who leave offerings at archaeological sites feel they are making a tangible contribution to the site's cultural heritage (2018: 118).

person is the thing' (2006: 63). This is a merge that anthropologist Alfred Gell terms the 'objectification of personhood' (1998: 74), which – through ritual deposition – leads to 'distributed personhood'. The ritual deposit, regardless of how anonymous it may seem, becomes a detached part, a 'spin-off', of the depositor (1998: 104).

Far more pages would be needed to do justice to the complex questions of the *where*, *who*, and *why* of 'ritual litter'. This Element is focused instead on the *what*: the deposited objects themselves, their materialities, and their seemingly contradictory designations as both 'litter' and 'heritage'. However, although this section provided only a brief overview, the *where*, *who*, and *why* continue to run throughout the Element alongside the *what*, deposited objects being so intrinsically bound up in the motivations of their people and the natures of their places.

2 The Material Culture

In his paper on historic votive offerings, Robin Osborne stresses the 'importance of the dedicated object' in exploring the beliefs behind a dedicatory practice (2004: 5). Ironically, even studies of material culture are sometimes guilty of neglecting the objects themselves, a point observed by historian Robert Friedel (1993: 42) and archaeologist Ian Hodder (2012: 39), both of whom advocate for the importance of studying the actual materiality of material culture. The aim of this section is to do just that. To think about what types of objects constitute 'ritual litter', why they were chosen by their depositors, and what it is about their materiality that deems them (to some people at least) appropriate ritual deposits. It will be left to Section 3 to consider what it is about these objects that makes them, to others, *in*appropriate ritual deposits.

There is a risk of overgeneralizing about the types of objects. Studying Mass Rocks in Uíbh Laoghaire, Ireland, Bishop notes: 'The range of votive offerings deposited at sacred spaces can vary enormously' (2016: 44), and they can also change over time and across sites. Spangen and Äikäs's (2020) repeated surveys of contemporary deposits at Sámi offering sites in Alta, Northern Norway, for example, reveal changes in the character of deposits and variations in objects across different sites within the same region. If the diversity of objects is notable even at similar sites within the same regions, how immense must it be worldwide when we also include wholly contemporary tourist assemblages and memorials?

Various studies have revealed types of objects very specific to the locale, purposes, or 'traditions' of a site. Many finds at coastal historic Sámi offering sites in Norway and Finland are related to fishing, such as lures, fishing rods, and nets (Äikäs, 2015: 164; Spangen & Äikäs, 2020: 317). The Cruz de Ferro, the iron cross marking the highest point of the Camino Frances in Spain, houses an assemblage of small stones brought by pilgrims from their myriad homes, identified by Groenewoudt as 'symbolically leaving behind something which burdened their soul' (2017: 19–20). While the majority of ritual deposits left in *Casa di Giulietta*, Verona – the purported 'House of Juliet Capulet' of Shakespeare fame – are related to romance, from heart-shaped padlocks inscribed with the names of lovers to letters written 'to Juliet' requesting relationship advice. Given the vast variety of ritual deposits being made world-wide, there is certainly no potential for drawing up a comprehensive list. However, some categories of objects do feature far more prominently than others.

Organic materials are particularly common, such as food and drink items. In Jutta Leskovar's survey of over 200 contemporary Pagans in Austria, the UK, and the USA, it was revealed that food and liquids were often deposited because participants, concerned about harming nature and animals, only wished to leave decomposable offerings (2018: 134). This decomposability makes it difficult to judge the extent to which perishable material is deposited, but what evidence there is suggests the custom features in many diverse contexts. Vegetal offerings are identified as particularly prominent at contemporary Pagan sacred sites in Brittany, for example, while Rountree recorded libations of water, wine, or milk and honey poured at sites of contemporary Pagan pilgrimage (Rountree, 2006: 99; de la Torre, 2018: 22). Blain and Wallis observed crumbs scattered during rites at the Bronze Age Nine Ladies stone circle in Derbyshire, UK (2007: 140), while at the Sámi ritual offering sites of Northern Europe, food such as bread, berries, meat, and eggs are popular offerings (Äikäs, 2015: 168; Jonuks & Äikäs, 2019: 22). Through ethnographic research, Doyle White sheds some light on the individual reasons behind such offerings. David Hicks, a middle-aged solitary practitioner, detailed in an interview with Doyle White how he has left crushed apple at sacred sites 'like a little sacrifice, a token of thanks in exchange for knowledge', while pouring a carton of milk over the White Horse Stone, a sarsen megalith in Kent, was a way of allowing the 'Wildfolk' to emerge (2016: 362).

Other natural ritual deposits are commonly reported: flowers, bundles of plants, bunches of sprigs, pinecones, stones, and shells. Although, as Äikäs recognizes (2015: 167), it is sometimes difficult to distinguish between items left by a person and those left by, for example, a squirrel, most forms of placement and arrangement indicate deliberate deposition. Most could have been opportunistic deposits: items sourced on site, indicating the depositors had not necessarily planned on making a deposit prior to visiting the site (see the discussion about 'pocket holdings' later). Even those that had been modified could have been spontaneous, such as the stones bearing written messages and the makeshift crosses constructed from branches deposited along the Camino Frances (Groenewoudt, 2017) or the dolls shaped from twigs recorded at Taatsi in Finland (Äikäs & Ahola, 2020: 171). However, some natural offerings were clearly sourced from or crafted elsewhere, such as polished and semi-precious stones, non-native plant species, corn dollies, and were thus planned deposits.

The reasons behind the selection of some of these objects are easy to infer. As much of contemporary Pagan spiritualism is connected to nature, it is unsurprising that stones, shells, flowers (their use as memoriam deposits is discussed later), and plants would be popularly employed in rituals. They are symbolically potent whilst being environmentally benign. And crystals and gemstones, while not necessarily native natural material, feature prominently in contemporary Pagan rituals, just as they did in numerous historic healing customs, because of the belief that they encourage positive energies (Bartolini et al., 2013: 380; McClean, 2013; Thurgill, 2014: 160). Consumables likewise have long histories of ritual use, food given as offerings to the dead, or drinks poured as libations to deities. In contemporary Paganism, foodstuffs are sometimes left purposely to be consumed by animals; 'In this way', writes Äikäs, 'the offerings return to the circle of nature' (2015: 168).

Although sometimes viewed as unsightly, natural and perishable deposits are not often treated as problematic. As will be explored in Section 3, it is generally the unnatural, non-perishable deposit that is classified as 'ritual litter', and the range of objects within this group are broad. Candles are particularly prominent, especially at sites held sacred by contemporary Pagan communities; Blain and Wallis describe them as 'ubiquitous tealights' (2007: 138). During her 2008 excavation at the Sámi ritual site of Taatsi, Finland, Äikäs observed twenty-nine burnt tea-light candles placed on the ground or on rock shelves. Äikäs and Ahola note the similarity here with contemporary Pagan activities in Britain (2020: 170). The fact that they were burnt is significant. It suggests that some candles at least may be evidence of ritual activity (the 'debris', as Rountree termed it (2006: 100), much like the drips of candle wax recorded at many sites), rather than ritual deposits in and of themselves. If candles are the material residue, the detritus, of ritual, then the term 'ritual litter' may apply more readily to them than other items.

The candle's popularity in rituals at such sites is understandable. They are often associated with contemporary Pagan rituals; their colour and sometimes shape or size are often held to be spiritually significant (Bartolini et al., 2013: 381). Even beyond contemporary Paganism, candles – much like consumables – are well-established ritual objects. From the candle in the sacrificial cake presented at the feast of the Greek goddess Artemis to the votive candle in a Christian church, from the candle symbolic of Buddha's light placed at a Buddhist shrine to the signifier of age on a birthday cake, the lit candle has a long history of ritual and spiritual significance (Shoham, 2021). In his study of candle-lighting ceremonies in Norwegian high schools, Johan Lövgren (2018) demonstrates the many (and inclusive) layers of a lit candle's symbolism even in secular contexts: as an expression of fellowship, for serenity and meditation, as an expression of self, and for the beauty of its aesthetics. The symbolism and ritual potency of the candle will be familiar to most people, regardless of their spiritual beliefs, and their popularity as objects at sacred sites is unsurprising.

Even more popular than the candle is the coin. They are pushed into the cracks of megaliths, hidden in natural holes or atop towering plateaus at Sámi ritual offering sites, hurled from mountaintops, tossed into fountains and holy wells, and inserted into fallen trees. Their prevalence as modern-day deposits reflects (and undoubtedly feeds from) their historic popularity as ritual offerings or votives. Deposited in a broad range of locations, from bogs, springs, and wells to temples, churches, and graves, they have become so synonymous with ritual exchange that Nanouschka Myrberg Burström, in her introduction to the multi-contributor volume *Divina Moneta: Coins in Religion and Ritual*, refers to them as 'material expressions of religion' (2018: 3).

Henry Maguire describes the coin as imbued with 'extramonetary powers' (1997: 1053), and its associations with luck and protection have certainly enjoyed a long history (cf. Hall, 2012; Houlbrook, 2018a: 44–55). Carried as talismans, pierced and worn on cords for protection, bent as charms against witchcraft, attached to helmets before battle, deposited on ships to ensure safe passage, and hidden in the corners of houses to attract good fortune are just some of the many methods employed through history to draw on the coin's 'extramonetary powers'. The coin has also widely been used in healing rituals, believed to cure ailments ranging from tuberculosis and epilepsy to rheumatism and skin complaints. In medieval England, folding a penny in half was a common sickbed rite, believed to cure the patient if accompanied by prayer (Finucane, 1977: 94). From the late medieval to the early modern periods, small gold coins, known as the 'angel' because they bore the image of the Archangel Michael, were given to the sick in the 'touching' ceremony. Patients ritually 'touched' – and consequently cured – by the English monarch would be presented with the coin to be worn around the neck on a cord, to ensure the disease did not return (Charlton, 1914).

In many contexts, these uses led to the ritual deposition of the coin. For example, coins (often bent in confirmation of a vow) were offered at the shrines of saints, in thanks for a prayer being answered (Walsham, 2011: 213). Coins were also frequently deposited when employed as mediums in healing magic, believed to transfer ailments from a person to a place or other object through contagious transfer (see the discussion about rags later in the text).[12] In the example of skin diseases given by Jonuks and Äikäs, writing of Finland and Estonia, a coin was held or rubbed against the inflicted skin and then deposited in a spring or placed on a stone, removing the ailment from the person and anchoring it to the place (2019: 15). Coins were, and still are, also deposited in or near holy wells, in exchange for cures from the presiding saints or spirits. The modern-day custom of tossing a coin into a fountain for luck or wish-granting stems from these earlier practices and magical thinking (Houlbrook, 2015a).

The coin's prevalence as a ritual deposit is clear, but, as Burström asks, 'What is it about these small pieces of metal that has made them meaningful within ritual use, century after century?' (2018: 4). There is no single right answer. The coin's material plays a role, with various forms of metal, such as iron, copper, gold, and silver, widely viewed as apotropaic or curative. The images they bore also contributed to the coin's perceived preternatural potency, with the royal effigy being viewed as particularly efficacious. The coin's more abstract, representational qualities are also significant, with no other object being so intrinsically linked with value and exchange. With many rituals following the same basic rules as an economic transaction – I surrender a coin and in return receive a commodity or service – it is unsurprising that coins are the most popular ritual deposit, offered in exchange for luck, protection, or magical healing. Convenience is also particularly important, with coins over the past two centuries having increased in ubiquity while having decreased in economic value. By the late twentieth century, in economically developed societies, coins of low denomination were common (and semi-disposable) items in most people's purses or pockets. The coin is thus a particularly convenient ritual deposit when a person chooses to make an offering spontaneously and so forms a significant portion of what Spangen and Äikäs refer to as 'pocket holdings' (2020: 317) within the context of ritual deposits (see later).

The rag or ribbon is another highly popular deposit. In Estonia, the use of rags and ribbons as offerings can be dated to the early seventeenth century; they were consequently adopted as ritual offerings by contemporary Pagan communities in the 1990s, claiming continuity with older customs, and later, tourists imitated the practice (Jonuks & Äikäs, 2019: 19). Rags and ribbons are also found in Christian contexts, tied to the crosses along the Camino Frances for example (Groenewoudt, 2017: 19). However, they are particularly common when the

---

[12] Contagious transfer is a subcategory of Frazer's sympathetic magic, whereupon a 'person is supposed to influence vegetation sympathetically. He infects trees or plants with qualities or accidents, good or bad, resembling and derived from his own' (Frazer, 1990: 39).

ritual focus falls on a tree. Trees either act as convenient altars within or near a sacred space or are seen as sacred in and of themselves, such as the (descendant of the) Glastonbury Thorn (Figure 5) and the Ankerwycke Yew. Rags and ribbons are well formed for attaching to the branches of such trees, which become known as rag trees. In Britain, rag trees commonly accompany holy wells and archaeological sites considered sacred by contemporary Pagans.

Rags were, and are, sometimes given as an offering of thanks, like the bowed coin deposited at a saint's shrine. If the saint of a holy well has provided a cure,

Figure 5 Rags and ribbons tied to this young incarnation of the Glastonbury Thorn, Somerset, England, 2013 (photograph by the author)

then the cured may leave a torn strip of their clothing. However, more commonly, the rag was viewed as integral to the cure as a medium of healing magic, again linked to the notion of contagious transfer. A person's clothing was believed to contain the illness of the wearer through physical contact and a metonymical link. If a strip of fabric was taken from the garment and attached to a tree, then the illness was believed to transfer to the tree, leaving the wearer cured (Hartland, 1893: 460). To some, there was the additional belief that as the fabric rotted, the ailment would fade (Bord & Bord, 1985: 59). To others, the curative spirit of a tree – which could be partaking in the sanctity of a nearby holy well, thus shifting from convenient alter to sacred in and of itself (Lucas, 1963: 40) – might transfer back to the wearer through the rag's metonymical link with them (Canaan, 1927: 104).

Rags taken from garments are popular ritual deposits because they can easily be attached to the branches of trees, but also because of their physical and metaphorical connections with their wearers. Unlike coins, which tend to be viewed as anonymous and alienable objects (although see Houlbrook, 2015c, for the conversion to inalienable object), many ritual deposits are chosen because of their personal nature. Jewellery and accessories are common examples of this, from rings, earrings, and bracelets to hair bobbles and purses (Figure 6). Like rags taken from clothing, such items may have been deemed appropriate offerings because of their close contact with a person. Toys are another example. A toy car, a soft toy, a Pez sweet dispenser, a toy brush, a trading card, and a toy ball have been recorded at Áhkku, a Sámi offering site in Northern Norway (Spangen & Äikäs, 2020: 317), while several children's toys appear to have been ritually thrown from the summit of Mount Diablo, California (Parkman, in press, see chapter 4). Toys may testify to a child's presence at the time of deposition or have been deposited on behalf of a child, perhaps one who is sick. The latter accounts for many of the toys, dummies (pacifiers), and children's clothing deposited at St Brendan's Tree in Clonfert, Ireland (Figure 7), believed to specifically effect the cure of children. Such items may have little economic but much personal value to the depositor, who is surrendering something of deeper meaning than a coin or candle.

Some of these objects will have been deliberately taken to the place of deposition with ritual offering in mind. Others, like coins, will have been 'pocket holdings': items that just happen to be on a person when they spontaneously decide to make an offering. Some seemingly random examples include a Polo mint at St Nectan's Glen, Cornwall; socks and various other items of underwear on the Munlochy rag trees of the Black Isle, Scotland (Figure 8); a yoyo and eyeglass lens from Sieiddakeädgi, Finland (Äikäs, 2015: 165); a lipstick, pen, and sunglasses at Áhkku, Norway (Spangen &

Figure 6 Hair accessories on a tree close to the site of a former holy well on Isle
Maree, Wester Ross, Scotland, 2012 (photograph by the author)

Äikäs, 2020: 317); locks and keys and eyeglasses at Mt. Diablo, California
(Parkman, in press); and cast-off shoes along the Camino Frances
(Groenewoudt, 2017: 21). The convenience of such objects do not necessarily
preclude personal significance though, and without being able to question the
depositors themselves, motivations remain obscure. The reasoning behind
a rubber duck left at St Nectan's Glen (Figure 9),[13] for example, is particularly
intriguing, as is the dustpan and brush deposited at St Brendan's Tree.[14]

The reasoning behind other deposits are explicitly stated, such as in letters
and written prayers found slipped between megalithic stones or wedged into

---

[13] Recorded during on-site fieldwork on 1 April 2013.
[14] Recorded during on-site fieldwork on 5 October 2012.

Figure 7 Socks, shoes, dummies, and hair accessories are some of the deposits for or by children at St Brendan's Tree, Clonfert, County Galway, Ireland, 2012 (photographs by the author)

trees. Such items may speak to deep meanings attached to the ritual of deposition but may still have been spontaneously made. Examining St Trillo's Well, Llandrillo-yn-Rhos, Tristan Hulse found that offerings of prayers, which had been left at the holy well since 1992, were often written on scraps of paper sourced from pockets and bags: the backs of receipts, used envelopes, pages ripped from diaries, transport tickets, and so on (1995: 33). Similarly, a detailed request for the ideal romantic partner was written on the reverse of a pharmacy receipt from the Czech Republic and rolled into a fissure of the Ardmaddy Wishing-Tree, Argyll, Scotland.[15]

The reasoning behind the love-lock, the most rapidly spreading ritual deposit of the twenty-first century, is also often explicitly stated. Words and symbols inscribed onto the padlocks, which are attached to bridges and other public structures, speak of romantic commitment. Lovers' initials and names, hearts and flowers, the occasional couple self-portrait, and messages of 'forever' are in keeping with the symbolism of the padlock itself: an object specifically designed to securely lock one thing to another (Houlbrook, 2021: 102–18). The deposition of the key into the water below, rendering the padlock irremovable, signifies the depositors' faith in the durability of their relationship. Some

---

[15] Recorded during on-site fieldwork on 2 September 2013.

Figure 8 The rags (socks, scarves, tops, and flags) draped over tree roots and tied to branches at Munlochy, the Black Isle, Scotland, 2012 (photograph by the author)

are clearly spontaneous deposits: purchased from nearby shops or hawkers capitalizing on the popular custom, such as in Paris, and inscribed with marker. Others, though, were professionally engraved or elaborately decorated, indicating that the couple had planned their romantic ritual deposit. However, not all love-locks are intended to declare and celebrate romantic commitment. Some, inscribed with messages of 'rest in peace' and 'gone but never forgotten', are clearly left in memoriam of lost loved ones.

Items left in remembrance form a large subgroup of ritual deposits, especially given the popularity of spontaneous shrines as outlined in Section 2. And while these so-called makeshift memorials appear random and chaotic, Grider

Figure 9 The rubber duck is one offering amongst the diverse range of objects deposited at St Nectan's Glen, Cornwall, England, 2013 (photograph by the author)

identifies a 'consistent basic "vocabulary"' to the assemblages (2001: 3), with Doss asserting that their materiality is 'highly scripted' (2006: 298). Doss further stresses that certain things are particularly effective at negotiating the complex emotional needs of grief. Flowers, the most prominent memoriam deposit, 'symbolize the beauty and brevity of life', while notes and handwritten cards 'give voice to the grief-stricken and permit intimate conversations with (and confessions to) the deceased' (Doss, 2008: 15). Along with photographs of the deceased, other elements of this 'vocabulary' include candles, religious paraphernalia, balloons, and objects in the shape of butterflies, as symbols of rebirth, or hearts, as symbols of love (Klaasens, Groote, & Huigen, 2009: 191). An example of the latter was the mass of crocheted and crafted hearts deposited across Manchester, UK, following the terror attack of 22 May 2017, in memory of those who lost their lives (Figure 10).

Memoriam deposits also often have personal meanings. Items that once belonged to the deceased may be deposited, from clothing to sports gear, and many objects are bound up in the identity of the deceased. Teddy bears and toys, for example, are appropriate memoriam deposits for children, signifying lost innocence. Patriotic symbols, such as flags, adorn the shrines of those who have died in war. University paraphernalia, such as caps and T-shirts, filled the campus shrines

Figure 10 Crocheted hearts were scattered across Manchester City Centre, England, as memorials following the Arena bombing of May 2017 (photographs by the author)

following the fatal collapse of the student bonfire at Texas A&M University in 1999 (Grider, 2001: 4). As well as speaking to the identity of the deceased, memoriam deposits can also, as Santino observes, 'index the nature of the relationship' between the deceased and the depositor (2004: 370): a high school jacket or football jersey may indicate a deposit from a fellow student; a dog tag may be offered by a comrade soldier (Klaasens, Groote, & Huigen, 2009: 191).

In the case of prominent figures, items associated with their character, hobbies, and habits are frequently deposited by fans, who demonstrate care in their choice of objects (Graves-Brown & Orange, 2017: 121). At the Eugene, Oregon, roadside shrine of long-distance runner Steve Prefontaine, who died in a motoring accident in 1975, runners and fans deposit running shoes, caps, T-shirts, bottles of sports drinks, and energy bars, in keeping with his occupation (Wojcik, 2008). Bottles of wine, cigars, and dog figurines left at the memorials for Dutch politician Pim

Fortuyn spoke to his lifestyle and beloved pet dogs (Doss, 2008: 30). Fans left cigarette packets at the shrine built to singer Amy Winehouse, a smoker, outside her former residence in Camden Square Gardens, London, following her death in 2011 (Orange & Graves-Brown, 2019: 352). While packets of marijuana and bottles of whiskey are left at the grave of singer/writer Jim Morrison at Père Lachaise Cemetery, Paris (Margry, 2008b: 164). Such items appear to be given in homage or as gifts to the deceased, who may be able to appreciate them in the afterlife. Other items left at such shrines speak of desired or perceived connections between the deceased and the depositor. Margry describes how a musician from Naples left a sheet of his lyrics on Morrison's grave, 'hoping to bring down success upon himself' (2008b: 165). While Daniel Wojcik believes that the many running medals, trophies, shoes, and socks worn during races deposited at the shrine to Prefontaine 'may represent proof of the "success" of Prefontaine's influence and are presented as a public gesture of gratitude, much in the same manner as the votive offerings left at shrines for folk saints' (2008: 230).

To conclude, the objects that constitute so-called ritual litter are so many and varied that drawing up a comprehensive list is unfeasible. However, surveying different forms of ritual assemblage identifies some objects as clearly more popular deposits than others, and certain artefact vocabularies do begin to emerge. Organic materials, from flowers to food, dominate, alongside coins, candles, and rags. Personal items are also prominent: objects worn close to the body or intrinsically linked with the depositor or, in the case of commemorative items, with the deceased. Given the variety amongst the depositors, from geographical to spiritual, it is impossible to offer a definitive explanation for why certain deposits are more common than others. But, in considering their materialities, it becomes possible to understand how these vocabularies are formed in keeping with the ideas, ideologies, and intentions behind the rituals, from communion with the supernatural to commemorative. Some deposits are planned, others spontaneous. Some are convenient, others personal. Some are perishable, others durable. Physical materials, abstract symbolism, and practical considerations combine to produce a diverse set of ritual deposits appropriate to a diverse set of rituals. Or at least appropriate to the depositors. The following section considers what it is about these ritual deposits that make other people deem them *in*appropriate and therefore 'litter'.

3 Deposits as 'Litter'

The ritual deposition of an object does not equate to the end of that object. Its biography continues beyond its moment of relinquishment. It may have been metaphorically sacrificed, but it has not been destroyed, and it continues to exist. It may now be inalienably linked to its depositor through the act of deposition (see Houlbrook, 2015c), but it is also distinct from the person who sacrificed it. It is a tangible object that, no matter how small, impacts upon its environment. It can continue to act on the senses; people and animals can see it, touch it, perhaps smell or hear it depending on the nature of the object. Maybe even taste it – though not recommended. Once left by its depositor, there are myriad paths down which its biography can travel. Any number of things can happen to it.

It could stay where it was deposited and decay out of existence. This process may take days, such as food; years, such as textiles; or centuries, such as metallic objects. Certainly, many (probable) ritual deposits have survived to us from history and prehistory, from coins hidden in the earth to swords left in rivers (see, for example, Bradley, 1990). Particularly durable items may remain in place, buried over time until the site is excavated by future archaeologists (an optimistic thought), the land is altered, or the planet destroyed (a less optimistic thought). However, many contemporary ritual deposits are not permanent fixtures. With some exceptions, most notably love-locks, the contemporary deposit is often unsecured or easily detached. Small and portable, they can easily be removed – and at some point following their deposition, many are.

Ritual deposits can be blown away by the wind or removed by local fauna.[16] Just as the edibles of the Canang Sari offerings are eaten by dogs and monkeys on Bali, animals such as rats, birds, and squirrels could be responsible for the moving or consumption of deposits elsewhere. Humans tend to be the prime culprits, though. In some rare cases, it could be the original depositor who removes the deposit. Love-locks offer examples of this. The concept behind the locking of inscribed padlocks to bridges is that the depositing couple can only part ways if the corresponding key is fished from the river below and the padlock unlocked and removed. It is difficult to judge how frequently this happens; after all, a removed deposit is rarely materially conspicuous. But the opportunity to diachronically record an assemblage in Manchester, UK, cataloguing its growth from seven love-locks in 2014 to over 700 in 2019, allowed the author to note the removal of at least eight, perhaps signifying the end of eight relationships. It is doubtful that the depositors/removers would have waded into the Rochdale Canal beneath the assemblage, so perhaps the key was retained rather than dropped into the water, or bolt cutters were used (Houlbrook, 2018b: 230, 2021, 64–5).

---

[16] For example, when a woman noticed that a stone she'd placed at the roadside memorial for her son was missing, she assumed 'that it had been blown away. I can't believe that someone would take it away from here' (Klaasens, Groote, & Huigen, 2009: 194).

In some cases, ritual deposits are removed by people other than the depositors because they desire the objects. During the early 1990s, archaeologist Brian Reeves recorded a variety of offerings made on Ninaistakis, a mountain in Montana perceived as sacred by the Nitsitapii (or the Blackfoot People): ribbons, tobacco pouches, shells, painted feathers, sweetgrass braids. Reeves noted that many of these offerings went missing over time, and while he acknowledged that some may have been moved by pack rats, he believed most were taken by (non-Nitsitapii) visitors of the human variety. 'It is possible', he theorized, 'that this vandalism is deliberate, in the sense that the people removing the objects know what their meaning is and why they were placed there, but it is more likely that it is done in ignorance [of their cultural significance to the Nitsitapii]' (1994: 285).

Desire for an object has also led to the removal of grave offerings. At the grave of Jim Morrison in Père Lachaise Cemetery, Paris, many fans believe that when objects come into contact with the grave, they are imbued with, to use Margry's words, 'sacred significance' (2008b: 151). So offerings ranging from letters and drawings to packets of marijuana are frequently taken by fans. As Margry observes, 'treating the dead with respect and the meaning of "property" are relative concepts for the fans . . . there are always fans who will jump over the barriers to appropriate something' (2008b: 151). However, a far greater proportion of offerings are removed by cemetery workers, who take them away 'as litter' at least once a week, perceiving them as damaging to the cultural heritage of the site (Margry, 2008b: 170 n). The current section is primarily concerned with this category of ritual deposit: the object that is perceived as 'litter' and consequently removed.

Here, the term 'litter' implies a negative assessment of the deposits as 'small pieces of rubbish that have been left lying on the ground in public places' (*Cambridge Dictionary*). This is not how many depositors view their offerings. As Section 2 demonstrated, there are often spiritual or emotional motivations behind the deposition of that particular object at that particular place. To the depositors, these items hold ritual value. But value is subjective, and as Spangen and Äikäs note, 'the distinction between ritual objects or offerings and litter can be fluid' (2020: 317). Why do some people deem these objects 'rubbish'? Why do they treat them as undesirable intrusions into a public space in need of removal and disposal, when to other people they are objects of ritual value? This section aims to answer these questions.

Environmental concerns are often cited justifying the removal of offerings. There is no denying that certain examples of ritual deposition have negatively impacted ecosystems. The scattering of ashes, for example, has reached such quantities in particular locations, such as the Lake District, that the custom has changed the local ecology (Frisby, 2019: 81). And ritual deposits are viewed as significant contributions to the pollution of the Ganges in India. Flowers, food, cremation ashes, candles, oil lamps, statuettes of deities, religious books, and clothing are deposited in the sacred Hindu river, along with residual soap from ritual ablutions (Alley, 1994, 1998). To the Hindu pilgrims and priests who deposit such items, they are ritual offerings. To government officials attempting to clean up a river already heavily polluted by untreated sewage and industrial effluents, they are additional, unwelcome waste. As environmental anthropologist Kelly Alley writes:

> The different interpretations . . . reveal the fundamental incompatibility between the views of pilgrim priests and government officials. The latter consider Ganga an ecological entity, see her power in terms of a wider physical or biotic environment and limit that power to the impact of human-created pollution; pilgrim priests see Ganga's power in terms of an imperishable force that, even in this age of degeneracy, staves off all sorts of human-induced assaults. (1998: 178)

Contrasting perspectives are also evident at European sites of contemporary ritual deposition. It is not often that the organic and biodegradable offerings, such as flowers and certain foods, are treated as problematic. It is the objects that will not so quickly rot, the non-perishables that leave a mark on the environment, that tend to be contentious (Blain & Wallis, 2007: 182). Tea-light candles are frequently disparaged as pollutants, as are plastic bags tied to tree branches in lieu of rags (Jonuks & Äikäs, 2019: 36). Coins are also notable offenders. In Martínez et al.'s 2020 *Environmental Pollution* paper, coins ritually deposited in natural bodies of water are held as sources of chemical and microbial pollution, with the potential to cause long-lasting contamination.

However, it is more often the historical and cultural heritage of a site, rather than its ecological equilibrium, that is feared at risk from modern-day deposits. Coins may seem small, innocuous offerings, but they can easily inflict structural damage. Visitors to the Rollright Stones, a series of Neolithic and Bronze Age megalithic monuments in Oxfordshire and Warwickshire, wedge coins into the stones following the belief that the local fairies will ensure good luck to anyone who makes a monetary offering. But, as Blain and Wallis note, 'it is damaging to the stone in which it is inserted, and its removal may cause further problems' (2007: 182). Likewise, coins have been lodged into the stones of the Neolithic chambered long barrow of Wayland's Smithy, Oxfordshire, by visitors since at least the 1970s (Grinsell, 1979: 68). This is a practice stemming from the belief, recounted in the eighteenth century, that mythological smith Wayland would shod a horse if both the horse and a coin were left at the site long enough (cited in Ellis Davidson, 1958: 147). Today, it is not Wayland who takes the coin but the National Trust rangers tasked with the removal of deposits. Speaking with the author in 2013, on-site manager Andy Foley described how he would regularly check for and remove coins from the stones. In the early 2010s, English Heritage even altered the site's interpretation panel, deliberately excluding information about the traditional custom of coin deposition in order to discourage the practice (Houlbrook, 2015a: 178).

Coins and ribbons were likewise frequently removed from the Wearyall Hill incarnation of the Glastonbury Thorn, Somerset. Said to be the offspring of the original hawthorn, which sprung from the ground when St Joseph of Arimathea struck it with his staff in the first century AD, it has become a popular recipient of contemporary offerings. Visitors deposit flowers and candles at the tree's base, as well as insert coins into its bark and tie ribbons, sometimes inscribed with prayers or messages, around its protective fence (Bowman, 2008: 251). Believing the latter two practices to put the previously vandalized (and therefore fragile) tree at risk, former Mayor John Coles took it upon himself to regularly remove coins and ribbons during the 2010s (Houlbrook, 2015a: 181–2).

At other historic sites, coin deposition is actively discouraged with signage. 'PLEASE DO NOT LEAVE COINS ON STONE AS IT IS DAMAGING THE STONE' reads a sign by a flagstone in Gartan, County Donegal. Not only is this stone originally part of a prehistoric burial mound; it is also where St Colmcille is said to have been born in the sixth century and is believed to cure loneliness (Ó Muirghease, 1963: 153). As such, the stone has been subject to coin deposition since the early 2000s. Noting that the coins discoloured the stone when it rained, the Colmcille Heritage Trust decided to remove all coins and erect the sign (Houlbrook, 2015a: 178–9). A similar strategy was implemented at the Roman Baths and Pump Room in Bath, Somerset. Visitors to the site had been depositing coins into the spring there since the 1970s, but concerned about the negative impact of a build-up of coins, management decided to discourage the practice. Coins were removed and visitors requested to deposit their coins in a designated bath instead, from which coins can be removed more easily (Houlbrook, 2015a: 180–1). Dispersion is a familiar heritage management strategy; to alleviate physical pressures on particularly popular tourist spots, brochures and information boards redirect visitors' attention to alternative, quieter areas (Timothy & Boyd, 2003: 174–5). Instead of crowd control, the strategy at Bath manages ritual deposition.

Just as there is evident polarity between these deposits being viewed as 'valuable ritual offerings' and 'disposable and damaging litter', these previous examples also demonstrate a schism in how the sites themselves are interpreted. To some people, these sites are sacred; they are platforms spiritually apropos to – indeed, spiritually necessitating – ritual activity. To others, they are secular sites of historic or cultural heritage value, in need of physical preservation. As

has been demonstrated at many prehistoric sites of contemporary Pagan significance, most notably Stonehenge (see, e.g., Bender, 1998; Darvill, 2006), when
these two viewpoints clash, conflicts can arise. However, it is not always the
case that contemporary Pagans leave ritual deposits and site managers remove
them. In fact, frequently, it is members of the Pagan community who denounce
the offering of non-biodegradable items and organize their removal.

Doyle White details several Pagan individuals and groups who not only
always remove their own ritual residue, such as candles, but also collect
items left by others (2016: 366). In order to protect the Rollright Stones,
local Pagans collaborated with the National Trust to clean up ritual deposits
and to provide education on the importance of conserving the site (Blain &
Wallis, 2004: 247). Pagan groups have also participated in the founding of
many conservation-minded groups, most notably the Ancient Sacred
Landscapes Network (ASLaN). This was set up in England in 1997 with
the mandate of facilitating the exchange of information about the care of
ancient sacred sites. Some of the many groups involved in ASLaN include
the Pagan Federation, the Order of Bards, Ovates and Druids, the Fellowship
of Isis, the Diocese of Oxford, and the National Trust. As is stated on their
website:

> Please take care when visiting sacred sites to leave them as the next visitor
> would like to find them. Respect the land and all its inhabitants – spirits,
> people, animals, plants and stones . . . If an offering seems appropriate please
> think about all its effects. Don't leave artificial materials. Choose your
> offerings carefully so that they can't be mistaken for litter. Please don't
> bury things. Please don't leave biodegradable materials that may be offensive
> as they decay. If the site is already overloaded with offerings consider the
> effects of adding more . . . In times past it was traditional to leave no traces of
> any ritual because of persecution. This tradition is worth reviving because it
> shows reverence to nature and the Spirits of Place.
>
> Don't change the site, let the site change you. (Ancient Sacred Landscape
> Network, 2014)

This same approach is evident elsewhere in Europe, where spiritual practitioners encourage the ritual deposition of perishable objects and disapprove of
the non-perishable, which are viewed as inappropriate and damaging to sacred
sites. In Estonia, for example, when the mass of plastic bags and ribbons were
removed from the Ilumäe sacred tree in 2009, it was the contemporary Pagan
group Maavalla Koda who organized the clean-up. The removal was respectfully ritualized though, with all deposits considered meaningful. The permission of the tree was requested before the offerings were removed (Jonuks &
Äikäs, 2019: 36).

It is not only contemporary Pagan offerings left at historic places that pose potential threats to the site's physical integrity. Love-locks are another modern-day deposit frequently denounced for the damage they can – and do – inflict to sites, specifically bridges. On 8 June 2014, a section of mesh along Paris's Pont des Arts collapsed under the weight of its love-locks, which led to the decision to remove them. So, in 2015, seventy-two tonnes (i.e. more than the combined weight of ten African elephants) of locks were bolt-cut from the Pont des Arts and Pont de l'Archevêché bridges. In Chicago, love-locks are systematically culled from the city's movable bridges by the transportation department, who deem the assemblages a 'public safety issue', concerned that the locks may fall onto boats passing below. While in Leeds, it was unease over some love-locks holding cables of the Centenary Bridge together, creating gaps large enough for children to fit through, which resulted in the removal of locks in 2016 (Figure 11; Houlbrook, 2021: 145–6). The concern demonstrated here is for people's safety as well as for the sites themselves.

Public safety has been cited as the reason behind the removal of memoriam deposits also. Items left in memorial of David Bowie on Heddon Street, London, for example, are regularly removed by the Crown Estate, the site managers, because they are viewed as a potential hazard for workers using nearby office entrances – although some were donated to the Victoria and Albert Museum (see Section 4; Orange & Graves-Brown, 2019: 353–4). Some road-side memorials are likewise removed because of perceived dangers to road users (Clark & Franzmann, 2006: 585). In the United States, twenty-seven

Figure 11 Love-locks being removed from Leeds Centenary Bridge in 2016 by Leeds City Council staff, England (photograph by the author)

states remove memorials if they pose a safety hazard (Dickinson & Hoffmann, 2010: 162), and they are often banned on these grounds (although see Section 4 for sensitivities towards memorials). However, the banning of roadside shrines does not seem to deter mourners, who widely and frequently establish memorials in defiance of official policy, with local authorities often looking the other way. As Chris Ross noted in 1998, 'in probably no other area of public life does public practice diverge so dramatically from official policy' (1998: 50). In 2010, this observation was made again by Dickinson and Hoffmann, stating 'there remains a discrepancy between policy and practice' (2010: 163).

Site preservation and public safety are two justifications for the designation of ritual deposits as 'litter'. A third reason is the desire to return a site to its prior, everyday uses (Arvanitis, 2019: 512). The large spontaneous memorial assembled in Brussels following the 2016 terrorist attack, for example, was eventually removed partly due to pressures of 'returning to normality', as Ana Milošević explains, coinciding with the reopening of Brussels airport and Maelbeek station Milošević (2018: 59). And the fourth reason is the offence provoked by the nature of some deposits. Some are perceived as rude and obscene, such as condoms deposited at the Glastonbury Thorn (Houlbrook, 2015a: 181–2). Others can be interpreted as cultural appropriation, with Spangen and Äikäs explaining that offerings left by non-Sámi at Norwegian Sámi sacred sites can demonstrate 'the borrowing of cultural elements from indigenous people without proper knowledge of their meaning' (2020: 317). Items left by tourists in imitation of indigenous tradition, for example, can be seen as desecration, with the secular intruding on a sacred space.[17]

Conversely, the sacred can also intrude on secular space. Complaints are sometimes made when religious paraphernalia is placed in public environs, such as crosses at roadside memorials (Dickinson & Hoffmann, 2010: 303). As Clark and Franzmann, who studied over 400 memorial sites across Australia and New Zealand, observe, 'The roadside is public, secular space, but memorial builders assume the authority to transfer this space into a sacred place' (2006: 588) – which not everyone is happy about. They detail a case in Ormeau, Queensland, where a nineteen-year-old boy's roadside memorial was removed and a note left in its place, which read: 'The community of Ormeau have endured this memorial site for one year and two months and we feel that is by far long enough' (2006: 588). Meanwhile in the USA, in 2000, a roadside memorial made of crosses in Colorado was removed by a local resident. When the family complained and the state became involved, the resident hired an attorney from the 'Freedom From Religion Foundation'. The attorney

---

[17] See Houlbrook, 2021: 151–2, for consideration of ritual deposit as 'tourist tat'.

successfully moved for dismissal by calling into question the legality of the memorial in the first place, which endorsed religion on public land (Doss, 2006: 303).

Memorials are often contested spaces, politically and spiritually (cf. Woodthorpe, 2011: 272; Frisby, 2019: 85). Sometimes, however, it is simply that the assemblage of items is considered unsightly. Three US sites, for example, remove roadside shrines that are, to use Dickinson and Hoffmann's words, 'considered an eyesore' (2010: 162). Another motivation behind the removal of the 2016 Brussels spontaneous memorial was its 'changed aesthetics' following deterioration of the deposits: 'Residents', Milošević recounts, 'started lamenting about the smell coming from the memorial after several weeks' (2018: 59). It was a telling observation made by Orange and Graves-Brown that it tends to be the memorial shrines set up in more 'upmarket' areas that are subject to complaints. Local communities put pressure on authorities to remove them if they are considered an eyesore. As Orange and Graves-Brown write:

> Stars such as Freddie Mercury and George Michael ended up owning homes in the more 'upmarket' areas of London, where neighbours, probably conscious of the value and situation of their property, are not entirely sympathetic to the memorialisation of former residents, except in the more 'official' form of plaques. (2019: 35)

Even within official mourning spaces, memorial deposits can be considered unsightly. Detailing the history of personal arrangements for group infant burials at Glasnevin National Cemetery, Ireland, Chiara Garattini explores the reasons behind the official decision in the 1980s to forbid individual decoration. 'The problem', she writes, 'was of an aesthetic nature (the chaotic array of objects, fences, and decorations is sometimes perceived to be in "bad taste")' (2007: 196–7). As with roadside memorials though, there was a discrepancy between policy and practice, with mourners continuing to decorate the graves with large quantities of toys and other items.

Aesthetics are behind many of the protests made against love-locks (Houlbrook, 2021: 146). The 'No Love-Locks' campaign set up in Paris by private citizens in 2014, its online petition attracting more than 10,000 signatures in support of a citywide ban of love-locks, was primarily concerned with reclaiming 'the historic bridges and beautiful river views that have been lost due to "love-locks"' (No Love-Locks, 2019). In 2015, Bruno Julliard, Paris's deputy mayor, was quoted as saying 'They spoil the aesthetics of the bridge' (BBC News, 2015), and love-locks as 'eyesores' is cited as reasons behind their removal from many other bridges, such as Dublin's

Ha'penny Bridge and Venice's Rialto Bridge. Members of the media have likewise railed against the aesthetics of love-locks, with *The Guardian*'s Jonathan Jones (2015) proving particularly disparaging. Declaring that the world's cities are suffering from a 'plague of padlocks', Jones laments that 'Europe's most beautiful bridges' are 'being destroyed' by 'visually repulsive' 'rusting clumps of metal'.

Aesthetics play a role in the contestation of ritual deposition in Lourdes, France. The Catholic shrine to Our Lady of Lourdes has received votive offerings since it was established in the nineteenth century, left as tokens of devotion and thanks to Mary. However, while certain offerings were encouraged by the church, such as written healing accounts and crutches, other objects – in particular, rags and the clothing of ailing pilgrims – were viewed critically. As early as 1864, a metal grille was installed in the grotto, and clerics ordered the removal of offerings to keep the site 'tidy' (Notermans & Jansen, 2011: 176–7). Today, written prayers to the shrine are permitted only in email form, and engraved marble plaques, commissioned at the site and officially installed, are the only offerings allowed. Any personal deposits left at the site will be promptly removed by cleaning personnel, while local souvenir shops have been ordered not to sell the votive offerings often commercialized at other pilgrimage sites (Notermans & Jansen, 2011: 179–80).

Catrien Notermans and Willy Jansen, who conducted fieldwork at Lourdes in 2004, remark on this disparity in how deposits have been treated. The miracle stories and crutches were uniform, as are the marble plaques today, and are thus permitted by officials who are aspiring to efficiency and order. On the other hand, 'a jumble of various objects would defy the shrine's aesthetic rule of homogeneity and orchestration' (2011: 178). Speaking to shrine workers in an office known as the 'ex-voto desk', Notermans and Jansen were told 'we cannot accept pilgrims leaving all kinds of personal offerings behind. Imagine that situation, how messy the place would be', a statement accompanied by laughter at the thought of the statue of Mary being decorated with the jewellery of pilgrims (2011: 180). Not all visitors are deterred by the policy, though (see Section 4). Clerical control of the site is resisted both overtly – notes, photographs, toys, and flowers are liberally deposited throughout the shrine – and covertly, with some deposits placed out of sight, such as beneath the altar cloth in the grotto (Notermans & Jansen, 2011: 181). Once again, the ritual deposit typifies the discrepancy between official prescription and actual practice.

To conclude, the ritual deposit becomes ritual 'litter' for various reasons. If it threatens the preservation of a historically or spiritually significant site. If it poses a hazard to a structure or to people. If it is viewed as offensive or intrusive, with the secular invading the sacred or the sacred invading the secular. And if it is considered an eyesore: messy, chaotic, and out of keeping with the aesthetics of a site. Once dubbed 'litter', the deposit can be justifiably removed. However, the removal of a deposit does not necessarily equate to the end of its biography. While many are simply disposed of without record, many other removed deposits have further life stages ahead of them. The next and final section details the various creative methods employed by site managers, local authorities, archaeologists, artists, and curators to explore and communicate the heritage value of ritual 'litter'.

4 The Deposit as 'Heritage'

Landscapes are mutable, their biographies complex, non-linear, and inalienable to the ebbs and flows of society. Since archaeologist Osbert Crawford first applied the palimpsest metaphor to the landscape of England in the 1950s, as a 'document that has been written on and erased over and over again' (1953: 51), geographers, archaeologists, and historians have been drawing on a variety of imagery to illustrate our complex relationships with perpetually changing environments. Simon Schama characterizes the landscape as strata of myth and memory (1996: 7), while Alexandra Walsham describes it as 'a porous surface upon which each generation inscribes its own values and preoccupations without ever being able to erase entirely those of the preceding one' (2011: 6).

So the landscape is a palimpsest, consisting of layers of meaning created and built upon by the generations of people who have lived and moved within it. And, approve or disapprove of them, ritual deposits form many such layers for many different sites. With the ebb and flow of society, these layers will eventually and inevitably be built upon and semi-obscured by new layers, but to dispose of an assemblage of ritual deposits without record is essentially erasing the tangible evidence of how thousands – millions even – of people have engaged with that landscape. It is deleting a part of that landscape's biography and dismissing a vital aspect of that site's heritage.

As this section frequently engages with the concept of 'heritage', a brief note is needed on how the term is approached, especially as it seems to elude tight definition, with Peter Larkham observing that heritage is 'all things to all people' (1995: 85. See also Lowenthal, 1998: 9; Harvey, 2009). For this Element, the mission of UNESCO forms the basis for an understanding of heritage. Their 1994 'Global Strategy for a Representative, Balanced and Credible World Heritage List' strove to 'recognize and protect sites that are outstanding demonstrations of human coexistence with the land as well as human interactions, cultural coexistence, spirituality and creative expression' (Bradley et al., 2004). The main question of this section is whether there has been recognition of ritual 'litter' as demonstrations of human interactions, cultural coexistence, spirituality, and creative expression.

Based on current thinking within the heritage industry, the contemporaneity of ritual 'litter' should not preclude it from being viewed as heritage. The time-centred criterion for attention and protection has been widely challenged, with organizations such as English Heritage having broadened their definition of 'heritage' since the early 2000s to include the contemporary (Bradley et al., 2004). If the sites and assemblages of the twenty-first century are recorded and preserved now, it is reasoned, then we can address our own heritage and legacy while it still survives. As contemporary archaeologist and heritage specialist John Schofield notes: 'Today's landscapes have the potential to become tomorrow's heritage' (2007: 2). The heritage industry, therefore, has begun to view modern-day landscapes in a different light; as not only worthy of preservation but in some cases in need of it.

Many archaeologists working on prehistoric/historic sites with contemporary ritual significance recognize this. Blain and Wallis stress the inclusion of modern-day ritual deposits in interpretations of such landscapes: 'Whatever form this material culture takes, it is clearly worthy of serious study, not only for issues of site conservation, but also in terms of the construction and performance of identity' (2006: 103). A decade earlier archaeologist Christine Finn, examining how Chaco Canyon, a prehistoric complex in the Southwestern United States, had become a focus for New Age ritual and deposition, stated, 'What should be classified as "junk" and how we deal with it at a time of broader acceptance of "other" practices are issues that archaeologists and those involved in heritage management should, I suggest, be considering' (1997: 178).

Äikäs and Ahola, writing of Sámi ritual sites, likewise state that 'archaeological sites do not freeze after their prehistoric or historical use; instead, the past and the present are intertwined at these places' (2020: 174). They advocate a site-biographical approach to the landscapes they study, recognizing the meaning-making processes that continue into the present day and are manifest in the ritual 'litter' deposited. Delun Gibby, working on the heritage of prehistoric sites in the Preseli Hills of north Pembrokeshire, Wales, makes similar assertions, opining that prehistoric sites 'allow an array of narratives to co-exist' and that contemporary ritual offerings 'bring an additional dimension to the interpretation and use of [a] site' (2018: 51–2). Most recently, E. Breck Parkman, Senior State Archaeologist for California State Parks, shares this sentiment, pointing out the need for care in what we label 'litter' and how we treat it, with deposits offering valuable anthropological insights into society both past and present (publication in press).

These archaeologists and heritage specialists practice what they preach. In the 1990s, Finn (1997), for example, was documenting how LoPiccolo, curator of Chaco Canyon, preserved the details of the vast range of objects deposited at the site for the future archaeological record by entering them into a database. Äikäs has been involved in several excavations of old Sámi offering sites where contemporary deposits have likewise been recorded. During 2017 fieldwork with Spangen, it was decided that the most ethically sound way of gathering data about modern ritual practices was to photographically document the deposits while leaving them in situ (Spangen & Äikäs, 2020: 317). Gibby (2018) has similarly produced a photographic record of contemporary ritual deposits in the Preseli Hills. While since 2008, Parkman has been publishing his archaeological surveys of the many historic and contemporary artefacts deposited from the peak of Mt. Diablo, California (publication in press). The details of 213 coins, ranging from 1920 to 2010, are published in a table,[18] while the myriad other items recorded are divided into the categories of accidental loss, intentional discard, and intentional sacrifice (with Parkman admitting that the divisions are often ambiguous).

In his vehement 2018 article, 'Human and Civil Rights, Archaeology, and Spiritual Practice', archaeologist Raimund Karl points out that archaeologists tend not to object to rituals conducted at 'their' sites so long as they do not tangibly compromise their integrity. However, if the rituals leave 'graffiti' or 'rubbish', then it is viewed as irresponsible destruction of a site that should be preserved for future generations. However, as Karl argues, if a site is protected 'in the public interest', then a reassessment of 'public interest' is needed. Spiritual practitioners – members of the public – have the fundamental human right to practice their religion in the ways they deem necessary. If those ways include the deposition of offerings at a prehistoric site protected *in the public interest*, then do archaeologists have the right to forbid or denounce it? 'It is no longer that we are right and they are wrong', Karl stresses. 'Rather, it is now that we have an opinion and they have an opinion, and some sort of consensus must be found that accommodates, as much as possible, both our and their wishes and opinions' (2018: 119).

However, as has been demonstrated throughout this Element, it is not a simple matter of archaeologist versus spiritual practitioner. Nor is it only archaeologists who are renegotiating the heritage 'value' of ritual 'litter'. Site managers and local authorities are also engaging with these issues, and it is not necessarily the case that prohibited or depreciated ritual deposits are simply disposed of by officials. In many instances, careful consideration is taken in the

---

[18] With many thanks to E. Breck Parkman for allowing me to preview this data prior to publication.

handling of such objects. For example, in their work on modern sacred sites in Finland and Estonia, Jonuks and Äikäs explain that ritual deposits are usually left in place: 'The leaving of deposits is usually justified with two arguments: the authorities do not know how to handle the objects, or all deposits are seen as meaningful and are thus left at the site. Removal has to be thoroughly argued' (2019: 36).

Likewise, many roadside memorials are left in place by authorities, even when such structures are classed as illegal. In the Netherlands, national guidelines state that a licence must be obtained to establish a memorial. However, Klaasens, Groote, and Huigen discovered that authorities are tolerant of unlicenced memorials: 'Governments are in doubt as to whether they have the informal, ethical right to interfere in matters that seem of so fundamental a nature to the bereaved' (2009: 195). In the United States, some local authorities only remove roadside memorials if they are severely damaged, while others allow them to remain for a set period of time (Dickinson & Hoffmann, 2010: 162). In fact, in New Mexico, a legislation was passed in 2007 making it a misdemeanour to destroy or desecrate a roadside memorial, while in Colorado, when a resident removed a roadside memorial in 2000 (as detailed in Section 3), the state charged him with 'desecration of a venerated object' (Doss, 2006: 303).

Ross, noting that 'Removing unofficial markers is a sensitive issue', detailed how in Florida road maintenance crews remove memorials but store them while attempting to contact family members, inviting them to retrieve the material (1998: 53). In fact, of the US states that remove memorials, only 7 per cent destroy them, while 76 per cent attempt to return the items to the family (Dickinson & Hoffmann, 2010: 161). An example in Australia demonstrates similar sensitivity. When major repair works were planned for a fifty-kilometre stretch of road in Victoria, the state transport authority issued the following statement: 'We are keen to talk with families who placed these memorials, to make arrangements for their storage, protection or relocation in accordance with family wishes' (cited in Doss, 2006: 303).

It is not only memoriam deposits that are returned to their depositors by local authorities. When love-locks are removed from bridges, many officials give their depositors the opportunity to reclaim them before they are recycled. Notices are placed on bridges informing people of the imminent removal of the assemblages, inviting the depositors to remove their own locks prior to the cull or to contact the local authority afterwards (Figure 12). This was the process in Munich, Melbourne, York, and Newcastle, to name just a few examples, while in Leeds bridge engineers made it even easier for deposit and depositor to be reunited. People emailed photographs of their love-locks, and the engineers

Figure 12 The sign erected on Leeds Centenary Bridge, England, warning of their imminent removal in 2016 (photograph by the author)

searched for them while removing them from Centenary Bridge in October 2016 (Figure 13). Once found, the locks were put to one side for the depositor to reclaim from the council offices or, in the cases of depositors living further afield, to be posted out to them. The fact that many people did go to the trouble of reclaiming their locks demonstrates the emotional attachment felt towards objects that are perceived by others as ritual 'litter' (Houlbrook, 2021: 75–6, 78–9, 92–3, 157).

Archivists and curators also play fundamental roles in the preservation of ritual deposits. As Section 3 detailed, votive offerings are strictly prohibited in the Marian shrine of Lourdes, France, and any that are deposited are removed. As Notermans and Jansen discovered, however, in the archives connected to the shrine is a curator 'who was said "to have a profound passion for the homemade ex-voto"'. This curator maintains a large collection demonstrating the immense variety of objects illicitly deposited at the shrine: prayers, poems, clothing, knitted items, human hair, photographs, paintings, toys, used bandages, crutches, and so on (2011: 182). Officially, the archives are not meant to accommodate the proscribed deposits, but 'convinced that these offerings needed to be saved and conserved', this curator defies protocol. She rarely meets the depositors themselves, and so details – names of pilgrims, dates of deposition, and personal stories – tend to go unrecorded, but as Notermans and Jansen demonstrate in their article, the preservation of these objects is invaluable for an understanding of how people interact with this site.

Figure 13 Leeds City Council staff matching the removed love-locks from the
Centenary Bridge with photographs sent by hopeful depositors, 2016
(photograph by the author)

In Verona, strategies have been employed to document and preserve ritual
deposits for nearly a century. The letters of heartbreak left at the supposed burial
site of Juliet Cappelletti (of Shakespeare fame) near Verona's San Francesco
Church have been collected and archived since the 1930s, when Ettore
Solimani, self-designated 'Juliet's secretary', was appointed by the city of
Verona as the custodian of Juliet's tomb. While, in 1972, the Il Club di
Guilietta (Juliet's Club) was set up as a non-profit cultural organisation run by
volunteers, dedicated to collecting and replying to the many letters addressed to
Juliet (Velazquez, 2016). Still, to this day, as their website states, 'Thanks to
Juliet's secretaries each letter is read, translated, answered and then kept in our
one-of-a-kind archive, that contains thousands of love stories and countless
words of love'.[19]

Items left at public memorials have also been collected and archived.
Doss affirms that 'memorials rarely feature precious materials ... Yet they
are increasingly regarded as unique, valuable, and irreplaceable collections
entitled to as much respect, preservation, and admiration as treasures
uncovered at ancient temples' (2008: 16). Objects deposited at the
Vietnam War Memorial, dedicated in 1982 on the National Mall,
Washington, DC, are, for instance, gathered up daily by the National Park

---

[19] Juliet Club. *About Us*. www.julietclub.com/en/su-di-noi/

Service (NPS) rangers. They are then collected by a museum technician from the National Capital Region's Museum Resource Centre in Maryland, archived chronologically by type, and then made available to researchers following submission of a research proposal (Grider, 2001: 5; Anderson & Donlin, n.d.). Over 214,000 objects had been catalogued by 2021, with the vast majority kept in off-site storage (Pers. Janet Folkerts, Museum Curator, National Mall, and Memorial Parks). As Michele Cloonan notes, this aspect of the memorial's care, which takes both a lot of time and storage space, was not planned or budgeted for by the NPS (2004: 35). As such, the NPS are by necessity selective in the items they collect and preserve, advising on their website that:

> Tributes left at the Vietnam Veterans Memorial are considered voluntarily abandoned property ... Items do not automatically become part of the museum collection. They are evaluated according to whether they fit the collection's scope ... Preference is given to objects with a direct connection to the soldiers listed on the memorial and to objects that have a discernible connection to service in the Vietnam War ... Items left at the Memorial are deemed to be the property of the National Park Service when voluntarily abandoned. Park staff may choose to save items for the museum collection or respectfully dispose of them.[20]

There is, in fact, a sixteen-page 'Scope of Collection Statement' issued by the NPS for the VVM. In this, the curator states, 'The collection is significant for its historical value; for its potential as a source for anthropological, historical, and sociological studies; for the motivations and stories behind the offerings; and for the ways in which the public has shaped the collection through its inter-actions with the VVM' (Anderson & Donlin, n.d.: 1). Deposits that do not become part of the collection, which are 'respectfully' disposed of, include mass-produced, impersonal, or perishable items; hazardous materials; objects that appear to have been left by accident, such as pencils and hats; and items relating to social or political movements not directly associated with the Vietnam War (Anderson & Donlin, n.d.: 13).

Following the seminal VVM collection, offerings left at other memorials began to be accessioned into museums. In 1999, following the Columbine High School shooting, over a hundred volunteers, led by the Colorado Historical Society (CHS), spent three days gathering up the items deposited at the memorial. In the 'Columbine Memorial Recovery Strategy Meeting' memo, members of the CHS were advised that 'We will save everything. Everything will be collected and removed from the site. Later decisions will be made as to how the

---

[20] www.nps.gov/vive/learn/collections.htm

mementoes will be handled. There will be no dumpsters. We need to be sensitive' (cited in Doss, 2008: 16–17). Perishable items were sensitively recycled, with rotted flowers becoming compost for local parks and fresh flowers converted to potpourri for victims' families. The remaining objects were archived, entering collections maintained by the CHS and the Littleton Historical Museum.

The same year saw another tragedy in the USA, with twelve Texas A&M University students killed by a collapsed bonfire. Anthropologists and archaeologists at the university adapted the methodology of salvage archaeology and undertook the Bonfire Memorabilia Collection Project. With inclement weather having already damaged some of the deposits, their work was viewed as urgent. Volunteers from throughout the community produced systematic photographic and video records of the assemblage; divided the area into numbered lots; collected and labelled each item; transported them to a warehouse where the wet items could dry out; and then placed them in boxes for storage (Grider, 2001). Four Bibles deposited at the memorial were particularly damaged by wind and rain and so were taken to the university's Archaeological Preservation and Research Laboratory, where they were carefully conserved. C. Wayne Smith and Sylvia Grider, anthropologists who worked on the project, explain the importance of such conservation and collection: 'In the future, these mementos will accurately reflect a collective expression of grief and desperation that cannot be expressed in words alone' (2001: 316).

Public institutions were called upon to save the temporary memorials blanketing New York City with candles, photographs, and toys following the events of 11 September 2001. Five million dollars of federal funding was issued to the Smithsonian 'to collect and preserve items of historic significance' directly related to the 9/11 attack, which included many memoriam deposits (Doss, 2008: 17). And in October 2001, a meeting entitled 'The Role of the History Museum in a Time of Crisis' was held at the Museum of the City of New York (MCNY), attended by representatives from over thirty institutions. As explained by James Gardener of the Smithsonian National Museum of American History and Sarah Henry of the MCNY, the main questions for discussion at this meeting were:

> First, how do we fulfill our obligations to future audiences and future historians by collecting and preserving the raw material that can tell the stories that they will want and need to hear and tell? And, second, how do we fulfill our obligations to current audiences by telling stories that they want and need to hear now, in the aftermath of these apparently history-transforming events?
>
> (Gardner & Henry, 2002: 38)

With the recognition that museums 'had an important place in the process of civic healing' (Gardner & Henry, 2002: 49), a steering committee was convened, and the agreement was made to avoid competitive collecting amongst the various institutions.

Such collection projects posed many challenges, raised many questions, and yielded many lessons. Some were practical. Whose jurisdiction did these memorials fall under? Who has the right or responsibility to assume the role of 'memory entrepreneurs' in this context, to use Milošević's term (2018: 57)? How can underfunded public institutions with limited resources adequately collect, process, and house these vast collections? How should such memoriam deposits be organized, recorded, stored, and displayed? How can the more ephemeral items be conserved? When only some materials can be preserved, what takes priority? It is often acknowledged that pragmatically, not all deposits can be retained. Photographic documentation is recommended as the most feasible solution to this, with Grider advising that photographs should be taken of memorials before they are dismantled and periodically to record changes (2001: 6). Schwartz et al. (2018), a team of collections and exhibitions professionals from Orange County Regional History Center, were tasked with the removal of spontaneous memorials for the 2016 Pulse Nightclub massacre in Orlando, Florida. They detail how, eleven days after the shooting, all deposits were photographed to form an online memorial, akin to one created in Paris following the 2015 attacks (Collins et al., 2020), but only some were salvaged. These were selected based on 'their unique nature, apparent significance, condition, and vulnerability to the elements' (Schwartz et al., 2018: 107–8).

'Are you keeping 10,000 items or 100 items?' was a prominent question in the mind of museologist Kostas Arvanitis as he faced the masses of memorial items deposited following the 2017 Manchester Arena terror attack.[21] When staff and students from the University of Manchester worked with Manchester Art Gallery to gather the items, the initial plan had been to collect only some. However, as Arvanitis explains, 'Very quickly . . . it became clear that the group did not have any strong selection criteria to distinguish the objects that should be kept and sent for conservation from those to be disposed of' (2019: 512). In the end, it was decided that everything would be kept; this was the only way to 'capture the scale of the memorial' (2019: 519; Figure 14). Some of the deposits were creatively repurposed. An estimated 2,000 soft toys were cleaned and then donated to charities; some of the candles were recrafted into 22 new candles to

---

[21] Pers. Comm. Kostas Arvanitis, Senior Lecturer in Museology, University of Manchester, 23 September 2021. I would like to thank Kostas for his time speaking with me and commenting on a draft of this section; I really appreciate it.

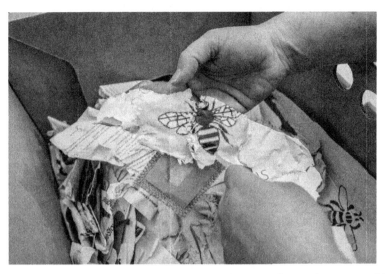

Figure 14 The bee, adopted as a symbol of Manchester, featured on many of the items left in memorial following the Manchester Arena terror attack of May 2017. They were all collected for the Manchester Together Archive (photograph by the University of Manchester)

be used in a church mass on the first-year anniversary and then offered to relatives of the deceased; potted plants were replanted around the city; and flowers were used for compost to plant 'Trees for Hope' (Arvanitis, 2019: 519, 527 n). The vast majority of the deposits, however, were sent to a restoration company and then housed at Manchester Art Gallery, where they remain today as the 'Manchester Together Archive'. A £99,700 grant from the National Lottery Heritage Fund received in 2018 has contributed to the documentation and digitization of more than 10,000 of its items.[22]

Some challenges faced by collectors are ethical. Beyond 'how can museums preserve these memoriam deposits?' is the question, '*should* museums preserve them?'. Removing offerings with the intention of saving them is still removing them, and preservation can be viewed as conflicting with a memorial's intended use. Loss of context is inevitable when spontaneous and emotionally charged public assemblages are boxed up in sanitized archives or put behind plexiglass in a museum, inaccessible to the public. And *when* should memorials be collected? To ensure sensitivity, a certain amount of time needs to elapse between a tragic event and the accessioning of a memoriam deposit, but this

---

[22] https://mcrtogetherarchive.org/

time is often at odds with the urgency of preservation given that these memorials are often open to the elements. Of particular challenge was the question posed by Gardner and Henry in the wake of the 9/11 attack: 'How do museums maintain critical distance without seeming cold-hearted? How do we remain compassionate without sacrificing the perspective that our institutions bring to the process of understanding the past and the present?' (2002: 50).

Questions such as this motivated the creation of the International Network of Archives of Spontaneous Memorials, which brings together individuals and organisations involved in such archiving from across Europe.[23] The purpose of the network is to facilitate the sharing of experiences and ideas, and one significant outcome has been wider recognition of the potential psychological and therapeutic impacts of such collections. On the one hand, by making these archives available for bereaved families and communities, they can aid the grieving process (Schwartz et al., 2018: 106; Arvanitis, 2019: 525). On the other hand, they can have a detrimental emotional effect on the professional staff tasked with dismantling and archiving the memorials. Archivists in Paris tried not to read the written messages they collected (Collins et al., 2020), and the professionals detailing their experiences of collecting after the Orlando night-club shooting recall the challenge of holding back tears until they were in the privacy of their homes (Schwartz et al., 2018: 112). Certain objects still managed to break through their defences. This was an experience shared by Arvanitis and his Manchester Together Archive colleagues as they collected and archived the Manchester memorials; they reached out to mental health hub Greater Manchester Resilience asking for help to 'process and manage those feelings'.[24] In a 2020 paper, Collins et al. maintain the need for more training and support offered to professionals in such situations.

It is not only memorials of death and tragic events that public institutions combine forces to preserve. In July 2021, when a Manchester mural of Marcus Rashford, professional footballer and campaigner against racism and child hunger in the UK, was offensively defaced following England's loss in Euro 2020, thousands of people covered the graffiti with positive messages. The assemblage of written tributes grew over the following weeks, but with a period of wet weather forecast, various institutions across Manchester – Manchester Art Gallery, Central Library Archives+, the People's History Museum, the National Football Museum, the University of Manchester Institute for Cultural Practices led by Arvanitis, and the Withington Walls Project – worked together to collect the paper tributes before they could be damaged by the rain (Figure 15). At the

---

[23] www.spontaneousmemorials.org/

[24] Pers. Comm. Kostas Arvanitis, Senior Lecturer in Museology, University of Manchester, 23 September 2021.

Figure 15 A collaborative effort between several organizations to gather the paper tributes deposited at the Marcus Rashford mural, Manchester, England, 2021 (photograph by Kostas Arvanitis)

time of writing this Element, they were currently in Manchester's Central Library's archives department for safekeeping, with talks underway regarding how the messages can be made accessible to the public.[25] Staff at the University of Manchester website explain that 'The hope is that by preserving the messages, they will be permanently available as an important reminder of this significant moment in the city and country's cultural history'.[26]

Many ritual deposits that are collected and preserved end up boxed away in archives, accessible only to researchers with the right credentials or people directly connected with the deceased. Some, however, find themselves on public display. For example, some of the memoriam deposits left at spontaneous shrines for David Bowie in London, archived by the Bromley Historic Collections, form part of a permanent exhibition in Bromley Central Library (Orange & Graves-Brown, 2019: 354). And while the vast majority of objects deposited at the VVM are held in a storage facility in Maryland, some items

---

[25] Pers. Comm. Kostas Arvanitis, Senior Lecturer in Museology, University of Manchester, 23 September 2021.

[26] www.manchester.ac.uk/discover/news/preserve-marcus-rashford-mural-tributes/

were displayed in the Smithsonian exhibition 'Personal Legacy: The healing of a nation' (1992–2003). Accessioned deposits from the memorial also feature in the museum's digital exhibition 'The Price of Freedom: Americans at war', with their details and photographs displayed online: 'Bottle of Jack Daniels', '6 Pack of Beer', 'Carton of Cigarettes', 'Wooden Cross with Barbed Wire', 'Note and Colt 45 Beer Can', 'Christmas Tree'.[27]

Both digital and physical displays were made of 9/11 memoriam deposits. CityLore, a folklore organization in New York City, photographed the temporary memorials that sprang up across the city and displayed them on their website.[28] The New York Fire Museum created a display of memorial material (Gardner & Henry, 2002: 50), while the Smithsonian's National Museum of American History held an exhibition in 2002 entitled 'September 11: Bearing Witness to History'. Some are still on display digitally, and the museum's website describes them as: 'Teddy bear left near the Flight 93 crash site in Somerset County, Pennsylvania. Lent by the County of Somerset, Somerset, Pennsylvania, honoring the passengers and crew of Flight 93'; 'This collection of twenty-eight photographs, taken by amateur photographer Doug Potoksky, documents the September 11 memorials and tributes in New York' (Object# 2002.0100); and 'This rescue helmet and vest were part of the Port Authority of New Jersey and New York Police Department memorial at the site of the World Trade Center' (Object 2002.0056).[29]

Love-locks are another example of ritual deposits entering a museum environment. Many love-locks removed from Centenary Bridge, Leeds (detailed previously), were displayed in an exhibition at the Ashmolean Museum, Oxford, entitled 'Spellbound: Magic, Ritual & Witchcraft' (2018–2019). The curatorial team chose to include love-locks because they aimed to demonstrate, through material culture, that magical thinking is prevalent today as well as in the past. In a gallery dedicated to the cosmos and medieval love magic, the love-locks adorned an entire wall, each one glued to a miniature shelf. And projected above them were the inscriptions from the locks interspersed with Latin and French inscriptions from medieval love tokens: 'Amor vincit omnia', 'Mon desir me vaille', 'LOCKED OUR LOVE ONTO LEEDS 05.07.16'. The latter example was the inscription on a love-lock displayed centre stage in the cabinet greeting visitors as they first entered the exhibition (Houlbrook, 2021: 164).

---

[27] https://amhistory.si.edu/militaryhistory/printable/section.asp?id=12&sub=4
[28] www.citylore.org
[29] http://amhistory.si.edu/september11/exhibition/highlights.asp; http://amhistory.si.edu/september11/collection/record.asp?ID=107; http://amhistory.si.edu/september11/collection/record.asp?ID=51

Some removed ritual deposits are creatively recycled. In Japan, for example, an estimated ten tonnes of brightly coloured paper cranes are deposited annually at the Children's Peace Monument, Hiroshima. Some are left by visitors, and others are posted to the monument's museum or the Peace Promotion Division from senders worldwide. As the City of Hiroshima website explains, these cranes 'are folded as a wish for peace in many countries around the world'.[30] The cranes are displayed at the monument, photographed by staff, and entered into the 'Paper Crane Database' – 'In this way', the website explains, 'your desire for peace will be recorded for posterity'. The paper cranes are then creatively recycled by non-profit organization Orizuru Hiroshima in the production of *hagaki* (postcards) or posters to, as their website states, 'convey the heart of Hiroshima'.[31]

Another example of the creative reinterpretation of removed ritual deposits is the work of photographer Sara Hannant. Taking part in a clean-up day run by Cornish Ancient Sites Protection Network at Sancreed Well, Cornwall, in 2013, she helped remove the offerings (primarily rags and clothing, or 'clouties') that were not biodegradable. Hearing that these deposits would be burned or buried, she asked to salvage them and use them in her work. With the rags as subjects, Hannant created exquisite photographs, which were on public display in her exhibition 'Numinous', Forty Hall, London, in 2015, and still digitally exhibited on Hannant's website. Alongside her photographs were a selection of rags, tied to branches and displayed in a vitrine (Hannant, 2021). Some time following the exhibition, Hannant buried the rags in her garden. As she explained, this work 'was inspired by the imagined wishes and stories embodied in the cloths and the role played by the forces of nature in traditional healing rituals'.[32]

Love-locks have also been artistically recycled following removal. Melbourne is a prime example of this, with the 'Love-Locks Project' established in 2015 following the removal of around 20,000 love-locks from the Southbank Footbridge. The City of Melbourne began working with arts organisation Craft Victoria to commission five local artists to incorporate the removed assemblage into the creation of new artwork. The pieces, which included a bell made from the metal of smelted love-locks to a large-scale necklace of locks, were put on display in the City Gallery in August 2016. Following the exhibition, the pieces were entered into a public lottery, with the proceeds going to the Lord Mayor's Charitable Fund and the artworks going to the winners. A similar project saw a staggering €250,000 raised in 2017 for three migrant and refugee

---

[30] Paper Cranes and Children's Peace Monument – 広島市公式ホームページ (hiroshima.lg.jp).

[31] Pers. Comm. Rie Nakanishi, Curatorial Division, Hiroshima Peace Memorial Museum, 3 June 2021; Oryzuru Regeneration Project Hiroshima (npo-jp.net).

[32] Pers. Comm. Sara Hannant, artist, 27 August 2021.

charities following the removal of love-locks in Paris. The most aesthetically pleasing locks were selected, divided into 150 bunches, and mounted on stands made from wood or recycled paving stone. They were then auctioned off at the Crédit Municipal de Paris to some very generous bidders seeking pieces of Paris's cultural heritage for their collections (Houlbrook, 2021: 157–62).

Ritually deposited coins are also philanthropically harvested. Most of the coins removed from historic sites, detailed in Section 3, are still legal tender, and are taken out of the ritual realm to be returned to the economy. The coins removed from Wayland's Smithy, for example, are donated to local charities, whilst at Bath and St Colmcille's flagstone, Gartan, they go towards the conservation of the sites. Coins retrieved from contemporary sites, such as shopping centre (mall) fountains, are also put to good use. In fact, wishing wells and fountains are sometimes installed with the express purpose of encouraging coin deposits, to be later donated to charity (cf. Dundes, 1962). One example is the 'intu Trafford Centre Fountain Fund', established in 1999 at a large shopping centre in Greater Manchester. The coins thrown into the centre's many fountains, primarily by children, are routinely gathered up by maintenance staff and donated to a different set of charities each year (Figure 16; Houlbrook, 2015a: 182–3).

Sometimes, a spontaneous assemblage of ritual deposits is converted into a formal, permanent display. This occurred in 2020 and 2021 with several 'pandemic pythons'. Also known as 'community pebble snakes', these assemblages are formed of individually painted pebbles. An early example of this was the 'Kindness Rocks Project', began in 2015 in the USA, which encouraged people to write positive and inspirational messages on rocks and leave them in public places for others to find. As the project's website explains, 'one message at just the right moment can change someone's entire day, outlook, life'.[33] The custom had already spread to the UK by 2020, but it was the COVID-19 pandemic and consequent national lockdown that saw its popularity soar.

As folklorist Sophie Parkes-Nield observed, writing at the height of the pandemic, 'It seems that during these dark times [folkloric practices] are being used to visibly brighten our communities. Many of us will have perpetuated these customs simply for something to do – particularly families desperate to occupy children' (2020). One such custom was the 'pandemic python', which saw people draw pictures and write messages of hope, solidarity, and thanks to the National Health Service on pebbles and place them out into the community. Assemblages formed as long lines, hence the moniker 'python', and rather than remove them, some local authorities or community groups have made them

---

[33] www.thekindnessrocksproject.com/

Figure 16 Coin deposits in one of the public fountains of the Trafford Centre, England, along with signage identifying the previous beneficiary charities of the Fountain Fund, 2021 (photograph by the author)

permanent features. At Cockermouth, Cumbria, an assemblage of painted pebbles started by a local seven-year-old girl in 2020 was preserved in cement as a lasting memorial to the NHS (BBC News, 2020). While, in Southport, the Ocean Plaza leisure centre secures public additions to the 'community pebble snake' on Southport Pier with glue (Figure 17).[34]

The aim of this section, or the Element, was not to criticize or question the removal of ritual 'litter', but rather to consider the more positive responses to

[34] Ocean Plaza Southport | https://www.oceanplazasouthport.com/whats-on/; I am grateful to Daniel and Eve Davenport for the use of their photograph.

Figure 17 Painted pebbles forming a 'pandemic python' along Southport Pier,
England, 2021 (photograph by Daniel and Eve Davenport)

contemporary deposits. As has been demonstrated, there is clear and widespread acknowledgement of the cultural heritage value of such assemblages.
Many different groups, from spiritual practitioners to site managers, from local
councils to archaeologists, from archivists to artists, have engaged sensitively
and creatively with these layers of meaning in the palimpsest of our landscapes.
And what has been demonstrated throughout the Element is the subjectivity of
'ritual litter', with stakeholders often in conflict over the interpretation and
treatment of these assemblages.

A disorderly accumulation of rubbish to one person may be a sacred assemblage of ritual deposits to another, such is the plurality of meaning. What has
been termed 'ritual litter' can be simultaneously vandalism of an archaeological
site, spiritual offerings, tributes of love and loss, acts of fun, ugly or offensive
intrusions into public spaces, material of social and anthropological significance

to be preserved for future researchers, sources of charity, and inspiration for works of art. Not one interpretation is solely correct, just as not one stakeholder is in the right where disputes occur. It is not only unhelpful to align ourselves with one side over another; it is misguided to even think there are distinct 'sides'. Rather, there are myriad heterogeneous individuals with myriad heterogeneous viewpoints, none more valid than the other. Recognition of this plurality should be the first step in our engagements with these contested ritual assemblages.

References

Äikäs, T. (2015). *From Boulders to Fells: Sacred Places in the Sámi Ritual Landscape.* Translated by S. Silvonen. Monographs of the Archaeological Society of Finland 5.

Äikäs, T. & Ahola, M. (2020). Heritage of Past and Present: Cultural Processes of Heritage-Making at the Ritual Sites of Taatsi and Jönsas. In T. Äikäs & S. Lipkin, eds., *Entangled Beliefs and Rituals: Religion in Finland and Sápmi from Stone Age to Contemporary Times.* Monographs of the Archaeological Society of Finland 8, pp. 158–80.

Alley, K. D. (1994). Ganga and Gandagi: Interpretations of Pollution and Waste in Benaras. *Ethnology*, 33(2), 127–45.

Alley, K. D. (1998). Images of Waste and Purification on the Banks of the Ganga. *City & Society*, 10(1), 167–82.

Ancient Sacred Landscape Network. (2014). ASLaN Sacred Site Charter. *Facebook*, 3 February. www.facebook.com/AncientSacredLandscape Network/

Anderson, L. & Donlin, J. (n.d.). Vietnam Veterans Memorial: Scope of Collection Statement. *National Park Service, National Mall and Memorial Parks.*

Arvanitis, K. (2019). The 'Manchester Together Archive': Researching and Developing a Museum Practice of Spontaneous Memorials. *Museum & Society*, 17(3), 510–32.

Bartolini, N., Chris, R., MacKian, S. & Pile, S. (2013). Psychics, Crystals, Candles, and Cauldrons: Alternative Spiritualities and the Question of Their Esoteric Economies. *Social & Cultural Geography*, 14(4), 367–88.

BBC News. (2015). Paris 'Love-Locks' Removed from Bridges. *BBC News*, 1 June. www.bbc.co.uk/news/world-europe-32960470

BBC News. (2020). Coronavirus: Painted Pebbles for Cockermouth NHS Memorial. *BBC News*, 3 June. www.bbc.co.uk/news/av/uk-england-cumbria-52896390

Beattie, M. (2014). A Most Peculiar Memorial: Cultural Heritage and Fiction. In J. Schofield, ed., *Who Needs Experts? Counter-Mapping Cultural Heritage.* Farnham: Ashgate, pp. 215–24.

Bender, B. (1998). *Stonehenge: Making Space.* Oxford: Berg.

Bender, B., Hamilton, S. & Tilley, C. (1997). Leskernick: Stone Worlds; Alternative Narratives; Nested Landscapes. *Proceedings of the Prehistoric Society*, 63, 147–78.

Bishop, H. J. (2016). Mass Sites of Uíbh Laoghaire. *Journal of Cork Historical and Archaeological Society*, 121, 36–63.

Blain, J. & Wallis, R. J. (2004). Sacred Sites, Contested Rites/Rights: Contemporary Pagan Engagements with the Past. *Journal of Material Culture*, 9(3), 237–61.

Blain, J. & Wallis, R. J. (2006). Representing Spirit: Heathenry, New-Indigenes and the Imaged Past. In I. Russell, ed., *Images, Representation and Heritage: Moving beyond Modern Approaches to Archaeology*. New York: Springer, pp. 89–108.

Blain, J. & Wallis, R. J. (2007). *Sacred Sites, Contested Rites/Rights*. Brighton: Sussex Academic Press.

Bocock, R. (1974). *Ritual in Industrial Society: A Sociological Analysis of Ritualism in Modern England*. London: George Allen & Unwin.

Bord, J. & Bord, C. (1985). *Sacred Wells: Holy Wells and Water Lore in Britain and Ireland*. London: Paladin Books.

Bowman, M. (2008). Going with the Flow: Contemporary Pilgrimage in Glastonbury. In P. J. Margry, ed., *Shrines and Pilgrimage in the Modern World: New Itineraries into the Sacred*. Amsterdam: Amsterdam University Press, pp. 241–80.

Bradley, A., Buchli, V., Fairclough, G. et al. (2004). *Change and Creation: Historic Landscape Character 1950–2000*. London: English Heritage.

Bradley, R. (1990). *The Passage of Arms: Archaeological Analysis of Prehistoric Hoards and Votive Deposits*. Oxford: Oxbow.

Brolli, M. A. & Tabolli, J. (2015). The Sanctuary of Monte Li Santi-Le Rote at Narce. *The Votives Project*, 12 July. https://thevotivesproject.org/2015/07/12/narce/

Brück, J. (2007). Ritual and Rationality: Some Problems of Interpretation in European Archaeology. In T. Insoll, ed., *The Archaeology of Identities: A Reader*. Oxon: Routledge, pp. 281–307.

Bruner, E. M. (2005). *Culture on Tour: Ethnographies of Travel*. Chicago: University of Chicago Press.

Burström, N. M. (2018). Introduction: Faith and Ritual Materialized: Coin Finds in Religious Contexts. In N. M. Burström & G. T. Ingvardson, eds., *Divina Moneta: Coins in Religion and Ritual*. London: Routledge, pp. 1–10.

Cambridge Dictionary. (2021). Litter.

Canaan, T. (1927). *Mohammedan Saints and Sanctuaries*. London: Luzac.

Caplin, J. (2000). Three Coins in a Fountain. *Money*, 29(6), 34.

Charlton, W. (1914). *Touch Pieces and Touching for the King's Evil*. Manchester: Richard Gill.

Clapp, J. A. (2009). The Romantic Travel Movie, *Italian-Style*. *Visual Anthropology*, 22(1), 52–63.

Clark, J. & Franzmann, M. (2006). Authority from Grief, Presence and Place in the Making of Roadside Memorials. *Death Studies*, 30(6), 579–99.

Cloonan, M. V. (2004). Monumental Preservation: A Call to Action. *American Libraries*, 35(8), 34–8.

Collins, H., Allsopp, K., Arvanitis, K., Chitsabesan, P. & French, P. (2020). Psychological Impact of Spontaneous Memorials: A Narrative Review. *Psychological Trauma: Theory, Research, Practice, and Policy*. http://dx .doi.org/10.1037/tra0000565

Conley, J. (2020). Voting, Votive, Devotion: 'I Voted' Stickers and Ritualization at Susan B. Anthony's Grave. *Journal of Feminist Studies in Religion*, 36(2), 43–61.

Crawford, O. G. S. (1953). *Archaeology in the Field*. London: Phoenix House.

Darvill, T. (2006). *Stonehenge: The Biography of a Landscape*. Stroud: Tempus.

de la Torre, G. C. (2018). Flowers on Merlin's Tomb: Heritage Management and Neopagan Practices on Archaeological Sites in Brittany (France). In J. Leskovar & R. Karl, eds., *Archaeological Sites as Space for Modern Spiritual Practice*. Newcastle upon Tyne: Cambridge Scholars, pp. 21–37.

Dégh, L. & Vázsonyi, A. (1983). Does the Word 'Dog' Bite? Ostensive Action: A Means of Legend-Telling. *Journal of Folklore Research*, 20(1), 7–8.

Della Dora, V. (2011). Engaging Sacred Space: Experiments in the Field. *Journal of Geography in Higher Education*, 35(2), 163–84.

Dickinson, G. E. & Hoffmann, H. C. (2010). Roadside Memorial Policies in the United States. *Mortality*, 15(2), 154–67.

Doss, E. (2006). Spontaneous Memorials and Contemporary Modes of Mourning in America. *Material Religion*, 2(3), 294–318.

Doss, E. (2008). *The Emotional Life of Contemporary Public Memorials: Towards a Theory of Temporary Memorials*. Amsterdam: Amsterdam University Press.

Doyle White, E. (2016). Old Stones, New Rites: Contemporary Interactions with the Medway Megaliths. *Material Religion*, 12(3), 346–72.

Doyle White, E. (2018). Around the Witches' Circle: Exploring Wicca's Usage of Archaeological Sites. In J. Leskovar & R. Karl, eds., *Archaeological Sites as Space for Modern Spiritual Practice*. Newcastle upon Tyne: Cambridge Scholars, pp. 182–94.

Dundes, A. (1962). The Folklore of Wishing Wells. *American Imago*, 19(1), 27–34.

Eade, J. & Sallnow, M. J., eds. (1991). *Contesting the Sacred: The Anthropology of Christian Pilgrimage*. London: Routledge.

Ellis Davidson, H. R. (1958). Weland the Smith. *Folklore*, 69(3), 145–59.

Fernandez, J. W. (1965). Symbolic Consensus in a Fang Reformative Cult. *American Anthropologist*, 67(4), 902–29.

Finn, C. (1997). 'Leaving More than Footprints': Modern Votive Offerings at Chaco Canyon Prehistoric Site. *Antiquity*, 71, 169–78.

Finucane, R. C. (1977). *Miracles and Pilgrims: Popular Beliefs in Medieval England*. London: J. M. Dent.

Fitzpatrick, P. (2011). Widows at the Wall: An Exploration of the Letters Left at the Vietnam War Memorial. *Mortality*, 16(1), 70–86.

Foley, R. (2011). Performing Health in Place: The Holy Well as a Therapeutic Assemblage. *Health & Place*, 17, 470–9.

Foley, R. (2013). Small Health Pilgrimages: Place and Practice at the Holy Well. *Culture and Religion*, 14(1), 44–62.

Fowler, C. (2005). *The Archaeology of Personhood: An Anthropological Approach*. London: Routledge.

Frazer, J. G. (1990). *The Golden Bough*. Vol. 1. London: Macmillan.

Friedel, R. (1993). Some Matters of Substance. In S. Lubar & W. D. Kingery, eds., *History from Things: Essays on Material Culture*. Washington, DC: Smithsonian Institution Press, pp. 41–50.

Frisby, H. (2019). *Traditions of Death and Burial*. Oxford: Shire.

Garattini, C. (2007). Creating Memories: Material Culture and Infantile Death in Contemporary Ireland. *Mortality*, 12(2), 193–206.

Gardner, J. B. & Henry, S. M. (2002). September 11 and the Mourning after: Reflections on Collecting and Interpreting the History of Tragedy. *The Public Historian*, 24(3), 37–52.

Gell, A. (1998). *Art and Agency: An Anthropological Theory*. Oxford: Clarendon Press.

Gibby, D. (2018). Tir Sanctaidd: Neo-Pagan Engagement with Prehistoric Sites on the Preseli Hills. In J. Leskovar & R. Karl, eds., *Archaeological Sites as Space for Modern Spiritual Practice*. Newcastle upon Tyne: Cambridge Scholars, pp. 38–53.

Graham, E. (2014). Waxing Lyrical on the Materiality of Votives. *The Votives Project*, 14 June. https://thevotivesproject.org/2014/06/14/waxing-lyrical-on-the-materiality-of-votives/

Graves-Brown, P. & Orange, H. (2017). 'The Stars Look Very Different Today': Celebrity Veneration, Grassroot Memorials and the Apotheosis of David Bowie. *Material Religion*, 13(1), 121–3.

Grider, S. (2001). Spontaneous Shrines: A Modern Response to Tragedy and Disaster (Preliminary Observations Regarding the Spontaneous Shrines Following the Terrorist Attacks of September 11, 2001). *New Directions in Folklore*, 5, 1–10.

Grinsell, L. V. (1979). Notes on the Folklore of Prehistoric Sites in Britain. *Folklore*, 90(1), 66–70.

Groenewoudt, B. (2017). Past and Present Meet: Contemporary Expressions of Faith Along the Camino Frances. In C. Bis-Worch & C. Theune, eds., *Religion, Cults and Rituals in the Medieval Rural Environment*. Leiden: Sidestone Press, pp. 13–24.

Gymnich, M. & Sheunemann, K. (2017). The 'Harry Potter Phenomenon': Forms of World Building in the Novels, the Translations, the Film Series and the Fandom. In M. Gymnich, H. Birk & D. Burkhard, eds., *'Harry – Yer a Wizard!': Exploring J. K. Rowling's Harry Potter Universe*. Baden-Baden: Tectum Verlag, pp. 11–36.

Hall, M. (2012). Money Isn't Everything: The Cultural Life of Coins in the Medieval Burgh of Perth, Scotland. *Journal of Social Archaeology*, 12, 72–91.

Handelman, D. (1990). *Models and Mirrors: Towards an Anthropology of Public Events*. Cambridge: Cambridge University Press.

Hannant, S. (2021). Numinous. *Sara Hannant*. www.sarahannant.com/

Hartland, E. S. (1893). Pin-Wells and Rag-Bushes. *Folklore*, 4(4), 451–70.

Harvey, D. C. (2009). Heritage Pasts and Heritage Presents: Temporality, Meaning and the Scope of Heritage Studies. In S. Watson, A. J. Barnes & K. Bunning, eds., *A Museum Studies Approach to Heritage*. Abingdon: Routledge, pp. 319–38.

Hodder, I. (2012). *Entangled: An Archaeology of the Relationships between Humans and Things*. Chichester: Wiley-Blackwell.

Houlbrook, C. (2014). The Mutability of Meaning: Contextualising the Cumbrian Coin-Tree. *Folklore*, 125(1), 40–59.

Houlbrook, C. (2015a). The Penny's Dropped: Renegotiating the Contemporary Coin Deposit. *Journal of Material Culture*, 20(2), 173–89.

Houlbrook, C. (2015b). 'Because Other People Have Done It': Coin-Trees and the Aesthetics of Imitation. *Journal of Contemporary Archaeology*, 2(2), 309–27.

Houlbrook, C. (2015c). Possession through Deposition: The 'Ownership' of Coins in Contemporary British Coin-Trees. In C. Hedenstierna-Jonson & A. M. Klevnas, eds., *Own and Be Owned: Archaeological Approaches to the Concept of Possession*. Stockholm: Stockholm Studies in Archaeology, Stockholm University, pp. 189–214.

Houlbrook, C. (2018a). *The Roots of a Ritual: The Magic of Coin-Trees from Religion to Recreation*. Palgrave Historical Studies in Witchcraft and Magic, Cham: Palgrave Macmillan.

Houlbrook, C. (2018b). Lessons from Love-Locks: The Archaeology of the Contemporary Assemblage. *Journal of Material Culture*, 23(2), 214–38.

Houlbrook, C. (2021). *Unlocking the Love-Lock: The History and Heritage of a Contemporary Custom*. Oxford: Berghahn.

Hulse, T. G. (1995). A Modern Votive Deposit at a North Welsh Holy Well. *Folklore*, 106, 31–42.

Jones, J. (2015). Love-Locks are the Shallowest, Stupidest, Phoniest Expression of Love Ever – Time to Put a Stop to It. *The Guardian*, 2 June. www.theguardian.com/artanddesign/jonathanjonesblog/2015/jun/02/love-locks-removal-paris-rome-florence-stupidest-phoniest-time-to-stop

Jonuks, T. & Äikäs, T. (2019). Contemporary Deposits at Sacred Places: Reflections on Contemporary Paganism in Finland and Estonia. *Folklore: Electronic Journal of Folklore*, 75, 7–46.

Karl, R. (2018). Human and Civil Rights, Archaeology, and Spiritual Practice. In J. Leskovar & R. Karl, eds., *Archaeological Sites as Space for Modern Spiritual Practice*. Newcastle upon Tyne: Cambridge Scholars, pp. 110–23.

Klaasens, M., Groote, P. & Huigen, P. P. P. (2009). Roadside Memorials from a Geographical Perspective. *Mortality*, 14(2), 187–201.

Larkham, P. J. (1995). Heritage as Planned and Conserved. In D. T. Herbert, ed., *Heritage, Tourism and Society*. London: Mansell, pp. 85–116.

Leskovar, J. (2018). Neo-Paganism and Sacred Places: A Survey in Austria and Beyond. In J. Leskovar & R. Karl, eds., *Archaeological Sites as Space for Modern Spiritual Practice*. Newcastle upon Tyne: Cambridge Scholars, pp. 124–42.

Leskovar, J. & Karl, R., eds. (2018). *Archaeological Sites as Space for Modern Spiritual Practice*. Newcastle upon Tyne: Cambridge Scholars.

Light, L. (2009). Performing Transylvania: Tourism, Fantasy and Play in a Liminal Place. *Tourist Studies*, 9(3), 248–50.

Lovata, T. (2015). Marked Trees: Exploring the Context of Southern Rocky Mountain Arborglyphs. In T. Lovata & E. Olton, eds., *Understanding Graffiti: Multidisciplinary Studies from Prehistory to the Present*. Walnut Creek: Left Coast Press, pp. 91–104.

Lövgren, J. (2018). Secular Youth and Religious Practice: Candle Lighting in Norwegian Folk Schools. *British Journal of Religious Education*, 40(2), 124–35.

Lowenthal, D. (1998). *The Heritage Crusade and the Spoils of History.* Cambridge: Cambridge University Press.

Lucas, A. T. (1963). Sacred Trees of Ireland. *Journal of the Cork Historical and Archaeological Society,* 68, 16–54.

MacCannell, D. (1976 [2013]). *The Tourist: A New Theory of the Leisure Class.* Berkeley: University of California Press.

Maguire, H. (1997). Magic and Money in the Early Middle Ages. *Speculum,* 72 (4), 1037–54.

Manchester Art Gallery. (n.d.). Manchester Together Archive. https://mcrto getherarchive.org/research/

Margry, P. J. (2008a). Secular Pilgrimage: A Contradiction in Terms? In P. J. Margry, ed., *Shrines and Pilgrimage in the Modern World: New Itineraries into the Sacred.* Amsterdam: Amsterdam University Press, pp. 13–46.

Margry, P. J. (2008b). The Pilgrimage to Jim Morrison's Grave at Père Lachaise Cemetery: The Social Construction of Sacred Space. In P. J. Margry, ed., *Shrines and Pilgrimage in the Modern World: New Itineraries into the Sacred.* Amsterdam: Amsterdam University Press, pp. 143–71.

Martin, E. (2018). *The Art of Dealing with the Gods: Balinese Women and Ritual Labor.* Anthropology Department Undergraduate Honors Thesis, University of Colorado Bolder.

Martínez, A., Di Cesare, A., Mari-Mena, N. et al. (2020). Tossed 'Good Luck' Coins as Vectors for Anthropogenic Pollution into Aquatic Environment. *Environmental Pollution,* 259, 1–10.

McClean, S. (2013). The Role of Performance in Enhancing the Effectiveness of Crystal and Spiritual Healing. *Medical Anthropology,* 32(1), 61–74.

McNeill, L. S. (2007). Portable Places: Serial Collaboration and the Creation of a New Sense of Place. *Western Folklore,* 66(3/4), 281–99.

Milošević, A. (2018). Historicizing the Present: Brussels Attacks and Heritagization of Spontaneous Memorials. *International Journal of Heritage Studies,* 24(1), 53–65.

Moccia, F. (2006). *Ho voglia di te.* Milan: Feltrinelli Traveller.

Monger, G. (1997). Modern Wayside Shrines. *Folklore,* 108, 113–14.

Moore, S. F. & Myerhoff, B. G., eds. (1997). *Secular Ritual.* Assen: Van Gorcum.

Myerhoff, B. G. (1997). We Don't Wrap Herring in a Printed Page: Fusion, Fictions and Continuity in Secular Ritual. In S. F. Moore & B. G. Myerhoff, eds., *Secular Ritual.* Assen: Van Gorcum, pp. 199–224.

Network of Spontaneous Memorials. (2018). Creating, Document and Using Archives of Spontaneous Memorials: Building an International Network. www.spontaneousmemorials.org/

No Love-Locks. (2019) *Facebook*, 23 January. www.facebook.com/pg/ NoLoveLocks/about/?ref=page_internal

Notermans, C. & Jansen, W. (2011). Ex-Votos in Lourdes: Contested Materiality of Miraculous Healings. *Material Religion*, 7(2), 168–92.

Ó Muirghease, É. (1963). The Holy Wells of Donegal. *Béaloideas*, 6(2), 143–62.

Orange, H. & Graves-Brown, P. (2019). 'My Death Waits There among the Flowers': Popular Music Shrines in London as Memory and Remembrance. In S. De Nardi, H. Orange, S. High & E. Koskinen-Koivisto, eds., *The Routledge Handbook of Memory and Place*. Abingdon: Routledge, pp. 345–56.

Osborne, R. (2004). Hoards, Votives, Offerings: The Archaeology of the Dedicated Object. *World Archaeology*, 36(1), 1–10.

Oxford English Dictionary. (2021). Litter.

Oxford English Dictionary. (2021). Ritual.

Oxford English Dictionary. (2021). Rubbish.

Parkes-Nield, S. (2020). Five COVID Customs Which Emerged During Lockdown. *The Conversation*, 3 September. https://theconversation.com /five-covid-customs-which-emerged-during-lockdown-146130

Parkman, E. B. (In press). Finding Sacrifice atop an Island in the Sky. In D. Gillette & T. Sanders, eds., *The Intersection of Archaeology and the Sacred*. Springer.

Penrose, S., ed. (2007). *Images of Change: An Archaeology of England's Contemporary Landscape*. Swindon: English Heritage.

Rackard, A., O'Callaghan, L. & Joyce, D. (2001). *Fish Stone Water: Holy Wells of Ireland*. Cork: Cork University Press.

Reeves, B. (1994). Ninaistákis – the Nitsitapii's Sacred Mountain: Traditional Native Religious Activities and Land Use/Tourism Conflicts. In D. L. Carmichael, J. Hubert, B. Reeves & A. Schance, eds., *Sacred Sites, Sacred Places*. London: Routledge, pp. 265–96.

Richards, C. & Thomas, J. (1984). Ritual Activity and Structured Deposition in Later Neolithic Wessex. In R. Bradley & J. Gardiner, eds., *Neolithic Studies*. British Archaeological Reports British Series 133. Oxford: Archaeopress, pp. 189–218.

Ross, C. (1998). Roadside Memorials: Public Policy vs. Private Expression. *The American City & County*, 113(5), 50–3.

Rostas, S. (1998). From Ritualization to Performativity: The Concheros of Mexico. In F. Hughes-Freeland, ed., *Ritual, Performance, Media*. London: Routledge, pp. 85–103.

Rountree, K. (2006). Performing the Divine: Neo-Pagan Pilgrimages and Embodiment at Sacred Sites. *Body & Society*, 12(4), 96–115.

Santino, J. (2004). Performative Commemoratives, the Personal, and the Public: Spontaneous Shrines, Emergent Ritual, and the Field of Folklore. *Journal of American Folklore*, 117, 363–72.

Schama, S. (1996). *Landscape and Memory*. London: Fontana Press.

Schofield, J. (2007). Editorial: Modern Times. *Conservation Bulletin English Heritage*, 56, 2.

Schwartz, P., Broadaway, W., Arnold, E. S., Ware, A. M. & Domingo, J. (2018). Rapid-Response Collecting after the Pulse Nightclub Massacre. *The Public Historian*, 40(1), 105–14.

Shils, E. (1966). Ritual and Crisis. *Philosophical Transactions of the Royal Society of London*, Series B, 251(772), 447.

Shoham, H. (2021). It Is About Time: Birthdays as Modern Rites of Temporality. *Time & Society*, 30(1), 78–99.

Siadis, L. M. (2014). *The Bali Paradox: Best of Both Worlds*. MA Thesis, Leiden University.

Singh, S. (2005). Secular Pilgrimages and Sacred Tourism in the Indian Himalayas. *GeoJournal*, 64, 215.

Smith, C. W. & Grider, S. (2001). The Emergency Conservation of Waterlogged Bibles from the Memorabilia Assemblage Following the Collapse of the Texas A&M University Bonfire. *International Journal of Historical Archaeology*, 5(4), 309–16.

Spangen, M. & Äikäs, T. (2020). Sacred Nature: Diverging Use and Understanding of Old Sámi Offering Sites in Alta, Northern Norway. *Religions*, 11(7), 317.

Thomas, N. (1991). *Entangled Objects: Exchange, Material Culture, and Colonialism in the Pacific*. Cambridge, MA: Harvard University Press.

Thurgill, J. (2014). *Enchanted Geographies: Experiences of Place in Contemporary British Landscape Mysticism*. Ph.D. Thesis, Royal Holloway, University of London.

Tilley, C. (2006). Objectification. In C. Tilley, W. Keane, S. Küchler, M. Rowlands & P. Spyer, eds., *Handbook of Material Culture*. London: Sage, p. 63.

Timothy, D. J. & Boyd, S. W. (2003). *Heritage Tourism*. Harlow: Prentice Hall.

Turner, V. & Turner, E. (1978). *Image and Pilgrimage in Christian Culture: Anthropological Perspectives*. New York: Columbia University Press.

UNESCO. (1986). Stonehenge, Avebury and Associated Sites. *World Heritage List*. https://whc.unesco.org/en/list/373

UNESCO. (1987). Chaco Culture. *World Heritage List*. https://whc.unesco.org /en/list/353

Urry, J. (2002). *The Tourist Gaze*. London: Sage.

Velazquez, A. (2016). 35 Millimeters of Love and Faith. *The Votives Project*, 1 December. https://thevotivesproject.org/2016/12/01/velazquez/

Wallis, R. J. & Blain, J. (2003). Sites, Sacredness, and Stories: Interactions of Archaeology and Contemporary Paganism. *Folklore*, 114(3), 307–21.

Walsham, A. (2011). *The Reformation of the Landscape: Religion, Identity, and Memory in Early Modern Britain and Ireland*. Oxford: Oxford University Press.

Weiner, A. B. (1992). *Inalienable Possessions: The Paradox of Keeping-While-Giving*. Berkeley: University of California Press.

Wojcik, D. (2008). Pre's Rock: Pilgrimage, Ritual, and Runners' Traditions at the Roadside Shrine for Steve Prefontaine. In P. J. Margry, ed., *Shrines and Pilgrimage in the Modern World: New Itineraries into the Sacred*. Amsterdam: Amsterdam University Press, pp. 201–37.

Woodthorpe, K. (2011). Sustaining the Contemporary Cemetery: Implementing Policy Alongside Conflicting Perspectives and Purpose. *Mortality*, 13(3), 259–76.

Magic

Marion Gibson
University of Exeter

Marion Gibson is Professor of Renaissance and Magical Literatures and Director of the Flexible Combined Honours Programme at the University of Exeter. Her publications include *Possession, Puritanism and Print: Darrell, Harsnett, Shakespeare and the Elizabethan Exorcism Controversy* (2006), *Witchcraft Myths in American Culture* (2007), *Imagining the Pagan Past: Gods and Goddesses in Literature and History since the Dark Ages* (2013), *The Arden Shakespeare Dictionary of Shakespeare's Demonology* (with Jo Esra, 2014), *Rediscovering Renaissance Witchcraft* (2017) and *Witchcraft: The Basics* (2018). Her new book, *The Witches of St Osyth: Persecution, Murder and Betrayal in Elizabethan England*, will be published by CUP in 2022.

About the Series

Elements in Magic aims to restore the study of magic, broadly defined, to a central place within culture: one which it occupied for many centuries before being set apart by changing discourses of rationality and meaning. Understood as a continuing and potent force within global civilisation, magical thinking is imaginatively approached here as a cluster of activities, attitudes, beliefs and motivations which include topics such as alchemy, astrology, divination, exorcism, the fantastical, folklore, haunting, supernatural creatures, necromancy, ritual, spirit possession and witchcraft.

Printed in the United States
by Baker & Taylor Publisher Services